YOUR BRAIN ON
SEX

YOUR BRAIN ON
SEX

HOW SMARTER SEX CAN
CHANGE YOUR LIFE

STANLEY SIEGEL, LCSW

ALYSSA SIEGEL, LPC, CONTRIBUTOR

sourcebooks
casablanca

This publication is designed to provide accurate and authoritative information in regard to the subject matter covered. It is sold with the understanding that the publisher is not engaged in rendering legal, accounting, or other professional service. If legal advice or other expert assistance is required, the services of a competent professional person should be sought.—*From a Declaration of Principles Jointly Adopted by a Committee of the American Bar Association and a Committee of Publishers and Associations*

Published by Sourcebooks Casablanca, an imprint of Sourcebooks, Inc.
P.O. Box 4410, Naperville, Illinois 60567-4410
(630) 961-3900
Fax: (630) 961-2168
www.sourcebooks.com

Library of Congress Cataloging-in-Publication Data

Siegel, Stanley.
  Your brain on sex : how smarter sex can change your life / Stanley Siegel.
    p. cm.
  Includes bibliographical references and index.
  1. Sex (Psychology) 2. Self-actualization (Psychology) I. Title.
  BF692.S448 2011
  155.3—dc23
                      2011027390

Printed and bound in the United States of America.
VP 10 9 8 7 6 5 4 3 2 1

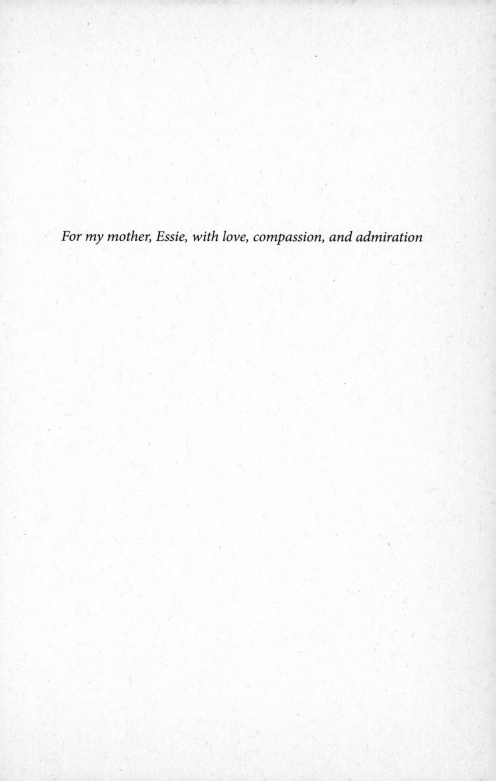

For my mother, Essie, with love, compassion, and admiration

The title of this book, *Your Brain on Sex*, is meant to catch your attention. Not just so you'll pick up the book, but because of this: it is your attention to sex that can change your life. I don't mean this in the ordinary sense of giving your sex life more attention. What I mean is that by focusing your thoughts on your true sexual desires, you can learn to understand what they mean and how you can use them to improve relationships, heal past wounds, and have a more fulfilling life. I use the word "brain" because what will be required of you is more than just physical or emotional. You will learn in this book how to think about sex intelligently so that your experience of it will organize your emotions, your body, your thoughts, your desires, your fantasies, and your spirit. *Your Brain on Sex* refers to what happens when all of these forces are engaged at full power. I call the process used to achieve this "intelligent lust." Following the steps described in this book allows the brain to organize all the information you have about a sexual encounter into an experience that is more than just good sex. It is not only great sex, but also smart sex—sex that can change your life.

Contents

Acknowledgments

I feel indebted to the many scientists, therapists, and artists over the years who had the courage to speak up about human sexuality and enrich our understanding of how sex acts as a healing force in our daily lives. It's through them that I came to appreciate the importance of sexual self-discovery as a valid goal in life.

I am deeply grateful to the patients who make an appearance in this book and who privately shared so much of their pain and triumph of their lives. I hope this book will honor them through the impact their stories have in helping others to celebrate their sexuality.

I am also deeply grateful for the guidance of my agent, Rebecca Gradinger, and the writer Gene Stone who both made important contributions in shaping the composition of the early manuscript, and to my editor, Shana Drehs at Sourcebooks, for her invaluable suggestions as the manuscript evolved. Thanks to social media consultant Adam MacLean and photographers James Meade and Posy Quarterman.

For their support, encouragement, and generosity, I thank my

xii   YOUR BRAIN ON SEX

colleagues John Heussy, MD; Bob Bergeron, LCSW; James Carnelia, PhD; and the writers Sheila Heti, Kathleen Cox, and Chase Booth.

Finally, I thank my friends and family—Wade Blackmon; Joey Smith; Richard Mancuso; Bob Ponterelli; Daryl Summers; Bridey; Lori and Mark Burns; Jeffrey Rose; and Judith Caneles—for their love and forbearance. I would have never been able to write this book were it not for the brilliant mentoring of the late Ed Lowe, my coauthor on two previous books, and my first editor at *Newsday*, Phyllis Singer. Of course, this book would not be what it is without the many extraordinary conversations with my daughter, Alyssa Siegel.

Introduction

> "*Sex lies at the root of life, and we can never learn to reverence life until we know how to understand sex.*"
>
> —HENRY ELLIS

If you're like most of us, the subject of sex makes you at least a little uneasy, if not completely uncomfortable. Sex is shrouded in so much mystery and secrecy and considered so personal that it's a wonder we can ever have an honest conversation about it. But if we could talk freely and openly with each other, we would discover that sex means something different to everyone, often something far from the ideas that Hollywood and Madison Avenue feed us.

Some of us think of sex as a simple act of physical pleasure, while for others it's a way of communicating deep feelings, and still others see sex as a spiritual experience. The definition of sexual activity also differs from person to person. It can be kissing, touching, intercourse, bondage, oral, conversational, punishing, dominating, wrapped in leather, romantic, observing, disciplining, and much, much more. It is as varied as our individual personalities.

But what usually doesn't come to mind when we think about sex is what is actually happening when we engage in it with a real person. Sex creates a moment of extreme intensity in which our entire inner life—our history and imagination—is expressed in actions. It is an altered state of consciousness in which the past and the present, body, mind, and spirit, all merge to form a new reality unlike any other experience in our lives. Depending on the circumstance, sex can be either physically and mentally gratifying or alienating and unfulfilling.

Because sex is so compelling at all these levels, it is frequently in our thoughts. I have been a psychotherapist in New York City for thirty-six years, and during this time, I have counseled innumerable patients. In nearly every case, regardless of the problem that led someone to seek therapy, the conversation has inevitably turned to sex.

Some patients express disappointment over the amount of sex in their lives, some are frustrated by a partner's lack of interest in sexual experimentation, some are concerned about sexual performance, some look in the wrong places to fulfill their desire, and still others are simply curious about their sexual fantasies and desires.

What I tell everyone, no matter what their issue, is that sex is more than any of these topics. It is a doorway into our deepest psyches. More importantly, sex can help heal our lives. By discovering our true sexual desires, as well as uncovering their origin, sex can be much more than just great. It can be life-changing.

This book will guide you to understanding your true sexual nature and show you how to use those insights as tools for enjoying smart sex, a kind of experience that will lead to personal and spiritual growth and a truly fulfilling life.

Why? Because true sexual fulfillment is based on self-knowledge and authenticity—not just the sexual act itself.

Here's my theory:

I have never met someone who has grown out of childhood without some conflict or unmet need. For most of us, the pain or unhappiness associated with these conflicts does not preoccupy our current thoughts and feelings, but does become part of our individual psychology, setting the stage for how we interact with the world.

As human beings, we are naturally driven toward self-healing, whether it's a small cut on our skin or a deep psychological trauma. Self-recovery enhances our chances of physical and emotional survival in the world. We are designed to do whatever we can to lessen pain.

At some point during the heightened sexuality of adolescence, we unconsciously eroticize these unmet needs or unresolved conflicts from childhood in a complicated attempt to heal ourselves. In other words, we turn early painful experiences into pleasurable ones in order to counteract their power over us. As human beings, we are driven toward reconciliation and catharsis.

As we grow into adults, these same conflicts, which now have sexual themes, are coded in our fantasies and desires or, in some cases, our sexual behavior. Through our sexuality, we attempt to gain mastery over feelings of powerlessness, shame, guilt, fear, and loneliness that might otherwise defeat us.

To help clarify this idea, here's an example from one of my patients: thirty-eight-year-old Sarah, the only child of unhappily married parents. Sarah's father, a warm and affable man, had failed in business as a contractor because, out of kindness, he often underestimated the cost of jobs, giving his clients bargains he couldn't afford. He also had a secret habit of gambling on weekends and, over the course of a few years, lost the family savings. Furious, Abby, Sarah's mother, never let her husband or Sarah forget this; Sarah was constantly compared to her father for her weaknesses and inability to assert herself in the world. Over the years, Abby's anger grew increasingly abusive.

Sarah secretly wished that her father would stand up to Abby's attacks and protect her—and himself. Instead, he withdrew from the family by sitting in front of the television for endless hours. Sarah felt abandoned by her father as he faded from her life.

During adolescence, Sarah daydreamed about sailors and sea captains and devoured romance novels with these themes. By the time she reached her late teenage years, like most boys and girls, she was flooded with confusing sexual feelings. Soon she was having sexual fantasies in which she was kidnapped by pirates, only to be later rescued by a strong and handsome sea captain. In her fantasies she unconsciously found an erotic solution to her childhood feelings of helplessness and abandonment by inventing a story in which she was held captive and finally rescued.

These fantasies reflect a common pattern. Not only are they enormously enjoyable but, enacted under the right circumstances, they can also counteract feelings of powerlessness, guilt, shame, fear, or loneliness, and, remarkably, heal old and deep wounds. By sexualizing unmet needs and childhood conflicts, we convert the pain associated with these experiences into pleasurable events. Our true sexual desires, such as Sarah's rescue fantasy, emerge out of an unconscious attempt to work through deep-seated feelings.

For many of us, our true desires (and their meanings) remain hidden from our awareness. When we are conscious of them, they are often shadowed by shame; we tend to think of them as deviant, perverse, or sinful because we do not understand their significance and instead internalize how powerful institutions such as religion and psychology have defined them. We police, deny, suppress, or keep our erotic lives secret. In the process, we disown an important part of who we are and who we could become.

The consequences of this denial can be enormous. If we do not understand our true desires, we can easily be lost in the dark. We may well choose the wrong partner. Or, if we act on lust alone without understanding the nature of our desire, we may mistakenly become attached to someone simply because we have great sex with him/her.

Likewise, if we choose a mate solely on the basis of personality or family background, we may attain stability or security, but sex can feel boring, empty, or, in time, entirely disappear from the relationship. Even when we do have a good time sexually, if we are not sharing our deepest desires and fantasies, we miss the opportunity to widen our vision and fully engage our true selves.

On the other hand, if we set out to identify our true sexual desires and the unmet needs or conflicts they serve to counteract, we take a giant step closer to wholeness. We lift our attention upward and create an experience of life based on self-knowledge and self-acceptance. From this position of strength, we can choose a partner with whom we create a sexual and emotional bond that satisfies our deepest needs. We can enjoy smart sex, and we can live in intelligent lust.

INTELLIGENT LUST

What is intelligent lust? It is a process in which we discover these true sexual desires. By that I mean we bravely explore what really turns us on and then begin to think about where those desires come from and what they mean. Then, perhaps the most challenging but exciting part, we use these insights to create a meaningful, satisfying, and healing sexual life.

How can we identify our true sexual desire and use intelligent lust effectively?

The answer, which can be found in the pages of this book, is not complicated. You will be given step-by-step instructions on how to discern your true sexual desires, interpret what they mean, access the childhood conflict from which they originate, better understand chemistry, honor and communicate your true feelings, and act out fantasies in healthy ways.

You will also learn how to use sex to create a "restorative relationship" with a current partner or a new one—a relationship that counteracts the failures and disappointments that many of us experienced in our families of origin and subsequent romantic relationships. By virtue of its mutual respect, honesty, generosity, and trust, such a relationship helps repair old conflicts and satisfies the persistent longing of unmet needs. It helps us reconcile past feelings that stalk the present, releasing us from long-ago dramas and allowing us to attain a more fulfilling future. We'll dive deeply into the specifics of a restorative experience in chapter 3.

Typically, people apply themselves industriously to school, work, friendship, health, raising children, and numerous other aspects of life. In the process of working hard, we acquire skills to succeed in these critical areas. With time, we can teach ourselves to become almost anything: a master cook, gardener, or tennis player.

But when it comes to sex, we leave it to happenstance or take a laissez-faire attitude. We expect sex to occur naturally without thinking or learning about how to succeed at having it. Even worse, there are successful movements to keep sex education out of the schools where young people can begin to explore their sexuality. And where courses do exist, the curriculum is so limited by conventional attitudes and political concerns that there is no true exploration of what sex really means. How can we be so fatalistic about it when sex is so central to our lives? There is so much to learn about sex and how we can improve it.

This book will take you through the steps that will teach you to become an expert on your own sexuality. Sex will cease to be shaped by fate and the universe. Instead, as you gain knowledge and learn to take action around your fantasies and desires, sex will take you deep into your body, emotions, and soul and deep into the tangle of relationships. Sex will become more intimate, open, trusting, and generous. And, without question, more fun.

More intimacy does not mean less autonomy. More passion does not mean less stability. In discovering your true desires, you open the closet door and take stock of all that's in it. You get to know yourself by observing what you've shelved or hidden behind other things. As the pieces of your erotic history and their meaning become clear, you become more authentic. Your fantasies and your actions begin to match because you can now reach into the closet without fearing what's in it and instead use everything inside to create a fulfilling experience based on your own preferences and style.

Sharing sexual fantasies with our partners brings us closer to them. By joining fantasy with reality, we create an experience of authenticity with our partners that exponentially strengthens the union. Smart sex goes a long way because it brings pleasure, meaning, and fullness to life.

There are many reasons why you may have chosen to read *Your Brain on Sex*. You may simply be curious about human sexuality and see the book as a resource for understanding its complexities. But more than likely, you are having concerns about your own relationship to sex. Maybe you don't feel good about it. Perhaps you're having difficulty letting go and enjoying sex—you feel self-conscious, embarrassed, or ashamed so you avoid it. Maybe you have trouble choosing partners with whom you are sexually compatible, and therefore your sexual experiences end in disappointment. You might feel detached from sex altogether and wonder why you have no interest in it. Or maybe you're unable to stop thinking about sex and worry that you have too much interest in it. Perhaps you delight in sex but stop short at orgasming and don't understand the reasons why. Possibly you're preoccupied with achieving an orgasm as if it were the only goal of sex. Certainly, some of you have picked up *Your Brain on Sex* because you're in a long-term relationship and rarely have sex anymore. You're worried about why this has happened and what you should do about it.

Whatever the specific reason that drew you to this book, you're reading it now because you want to improve your sexual experience. You want to feel better about sex and about yourself. *Your Brain on Sex* will help you achieve these goals. It holds the key to understanding your sexuality and to achieving a more authentic and fulfilling sexual life.

Just as we take into account such variables as religion, family background, and education in choosing a perspective mate, sexual compatibility should be high on the list of considerations. Ideally, this process of self-discovery that takes place by following the steps of intelligent lust should happen before we choose a partner with whom we make a lifetime commitment.

When we undertake a fearless personal inventory of our desires and their origins, we will learn what it is we are truly attracted to and what would constitute the maximum level of sexual compatibility with a partner.

But many of us are already in committed relationships. In no way should this prevent us from embarking on this journey. Instead, we should enter it with eyes open, aware that discovering our sexuality through the steps of intelligent lust can challenge the stability of the relationship, particularly if a partner is unwilling to embark on a similar journey. A partner may fear that discussing sexual desires may be hurtful and create distance and thus refuse or avoid it. In fact, the opposite often proves to be true. We must do our best to involve our partner in the process. Ideally, *Your Brain on Sex* should be read together.

But single or coupled, the initial steps are meant to be undertaken independently. When you reach step 5 (chapter 8), you will be shown how to share your discoveries with a partner, long-term or not.

Part I, Introducing Intelligent Lust, will provide you with the road map for examining your *true* sexuality. It will give you the tools and constant support to reach below what you know about your sexuality and bring your subconscious thoughts and feelings to the surface. You'll learn about the power of sex and its ability to heal old wounds and satisfy unmet needs.

Step 1, Getting in the Right Frame of Mind, will prepare you for the journey. Having the right attitude is essential to healing your sexual life. You'll learn how to open your mind to your deepest thoughts and to get past social taboos and psychological prohibitions that cause you to limit your sexual experience. It will help you put aside what you have been told is "normal" and discover what your real sexuality is beyond the prescribed conventions you may feel compelled to follow. You'll be instructed to keep a journal that you can use to record your insights and monitor your progress toward a more meaningful and satisfying sexual life.

Step 2, Identifying Fantasies and True Desires, helps you recognize your deepest desires as they are revealed through your sexual fantasies. By answering the questions in this section, you'll begin to recognize what actually interests you sexually and perhaps even put into words desires that you have been afraid to acknowledge before. Descriptions of other people's fantasies are included here because we often see ourselves in other people's stories. You may recognize your fantasies and sort out their themes by comparing them to the ones described. You might even find yourself aroused or completely turned off by some of these stories, which will serve as a clue about what your true desire might be.

Step 3, The Meaning and Purpose of Desires: What Our Fantasies Say about Our Past, might be the most challenging. Most of us are mystified about where our sexual desires come from and how they were formed. We may wonder whether they have any particular meaning or significance in our lives. Why do we prefer certain kinds of sex? Why do we like sex that is rough versus sensual? Oral versus genital? Why do we get off on being dominant or submissive?

We learn a lot about sex as children from social institutions such as churches and schools and later in conversations with our peers and from the media. But nothing influences our sexuality more than our families and what we learn from them. What we sexualize is far from random. Behind every sexual desire is an unmet need or conflict that grew out of our childhood experiences. Our desires represent an unconscious attempt to counteract the feelings associated with these conflicts. This is a difficult concept to get our minds around. Step 3 provides examples of the types of unmet needs and conflicts that many of us experience in our childhoods. It teaches us to identify the feelings below these conflicts and to understand the ways we might have converted them into pleasurable sexual desires in an effort to heal ourselves from the pain these old conflicts continue to bring us as adults. By comparing your own experience with the family dynamics described in the case examples as well as by answering the questions asked in this chapter, you will be able to map the relationship between your history, your current feelings, and your true sexuality.

Chemistry is not as much of a mystery as most of us think. Once we've identified our true desires and their meaning and purpose in our lives, we will be able to make sense of our attractions to other people. Step 4, Cracking the Code of Sexual Chemistry, helps us identify exactly what turns us on or off about another person. We learn why tattoos, for instance, or blond hair excite us and unmarked skin or dark hair don't. Here we will understand the specifics of chemistry, and the exercises provided will help us actually connect our ideas about attraction to the real people we come across in our daily lives.

While the first four steps of intelligent lust involve solitary explorations of our hidden thoughts and feelings, steps 5 and 6 involve a connection to other people. With our eyes now opened, we can begin to apply what we've discovered about ourselves to actual situations with partners.

Knowing with whom we are sexually compatible is essential to choosing the right partner—someone with whom we can be honest and open and with whom we can form the "restorative relationship" that is essential to healing old conflicts, satisfying unmet needs, and improving our chances of sexual gratification. Step 5, Determining Sexual Compatibility, teaches how to find out if a potential partner will meet or disappoint our expectations whether we want a short-term affair or a long-term relationship. The questions and exercises in this step challenge us to be direct, open, honest, and generous with potential partners as well as show how to determine their capacity to do the same. It calls into question typical dating protocol and offers a new direction for more authentic dating experiences. This step teaches us what makes us compatible with someone on multiple levels and how we can join with a partner in an effort to help correct past relationships and heal old wounds and at the same time enjoy amazing sex.

If you are already in a committed relationship, this is where you will learn how to share what you have discovered about your sexuality with your partner. Up until this point, it's been an independent exploration. If your partner has been following the steps as well, it's also the time for him to discuss with you what he has learned. The information in this chapter will guide you in integrating your partner into the world of your true desires. (Those of you whose partners haven't joined you on the journey or who you suspect may not share your sexual preferences can skip this step and jump ahead to chapter 10, When You're in a Committed Relationship and You're Not Sexually Compatible. You may have the chance to return to it later.)

Having established our "theoretical" sexual compatibility with a potential or long-term partner through the exercises in step 5, we come to a whole new level of interaction in step 6—Acting Out Sexual Fantasies. Here, actions speak louder than words. Through the exercises suggested in this chapter, we bring into alignment what we have discovered about our true sexual preferences with actual sexual experiences by physically enacting our desires with a partner. The exercises prepare us for sexual encounters rich with opportunities for engaging our innermost fantasies and preferences. Body, mind, and soul are merged through action, creating a level of authenticity within ourselves and with another person never previously achieved in sex. Achieving greater confidence in who you are takes away the fear of losing yourself in your partner's needs and desires. You *want* to satisfy his needs while taking care of your own at the same time. Whatever your past reasons might have been, you no longer worry about being overwhelmed or smothered by a partner, or have a need to retreat because you feel secure enough in who you are to surrender to the passion of the moment.

This is what turns great sex into smart sex. By that I mean sex that is driven by self-knowledge and self-esteem, two of the fundamental goals of intelligent lust.

In completing the steps of intelligent lust, we've changed. We feel better not only about our sexuality but also about who we are as people. We understand the profound connections between our past and our present and have a strong sense of our future goals for sexual self-actualization. And if we are in a relationship, we've learned how to use sex to improve it.

Part II, Living with Intelligent Lust, will give you the opportunity to deepen your understanding of your sexual experience by focusing on the particulars of your circumstance. If you're in a committed relationship, you'll find advice here. What do you do if you're not sexually compatible with your longtime partner? What if you have no interest in sex or the opposite, you're sexually compulsive? You'll find answers to some of these difficult questions in this section.

Chapter 10, When You're In a Committed Relationship and You're Not Sexually Compatible, will provide specific guidance for how to integrate a partner into the life of your true sexual desires. Through case examples, it will also show how different couples handle differences in sexual desires. But what do you do when you're in a long-term relationship and you discover you're not at all sexually compatible? This chapter includes some suggestions.

Successfully forging a relationship based on respect, honesty, trust, openness, and generosity by following the steps of intelligent lust better prepares us for dealing with the issues and crises that typically occur in relationships over time. Chapter 11, The Advantage of Sex, emphasizes the importance of making smart sex a priority. It highlights the advantages of such a "restorative relationship." A dramatic case example demonstrates the trust and strength a couple can have in dealing with an unexpected blow to their relationship.

Some of you are reading *Your Brain on Sex* because you are concerned about specific problems such as a lack of sexual interest, too much interest in sex, or the combination of sex with alcohol and drugs. Chapter 12, When Enjoying Sex Seems beyond Your Control, will help you understand the possible reasons for these problems and offer recommendations for handling them. You may indeed want to read that chapter first.

My intention for you in following the steps of intelligent lust is not to idealize smart sex, but instead to realize it. How quickly you succeed in getting there will depend, of course, on the speed at which you travel. Moving too slow or too fast has its risks, and of course, no journey is without some detours and obstructions. You will intuitively know what you can handle and exactly when. Trust yourself. In the end, you will be grateful for what you've learned, the changes you've made, and the promise of a more fulfilling future.

Psychotherapy is as much an art as a science. Within the context of a given theoretical model, clinician individual, styles emerge over numerous years of practice in which they learn the strengths and limitations of their ideas as well as the personal qualities they exercise to implement those theories. I have discovered over a long time that the best therapy is a reciprocal experience in which both the therapist and patient are transformed by the process. The case stories that populate this book are taken from my thirty-six years of practice. While I use them to illustrate and dramatize the ideas proposed in this book, it was also through the richness of each encounter with these patients that I was able to formulate and codify my thinking into the map that I offer you in the pages.

Because the personal background of any therapist—age, gender, religious beliefs, sexual orientation, and other factors—heavily influences his or her thoughts and actions and consequently his or her general approach to therapy, I have always found it useful to consult with colleagues whose backgrounds differ widely from my own. In evolving my ideas about intelligent lust, I discussed theories, presented cases, and even succeeded in getting some colleagues to follow the steps of intelligent lust themselves. Our discussions helped me expand and modify my original ideas to include what I present to you now.

In recent years, I have also delighted in the opportunity to engage in regular conversations about therapy with my daughter Alyssa, a licensed professional counselor in Portland, Oregon.

I am fortunate to have a colleague who knows me well and also feels comfortable enough to question and even challenge my thinking where other colleagues might not. As much as I could share the experience I gained from thirty-six years of practice, Alyssa could introduce me to the latest scientific thinking and research as well as, with freshness and excitement, her own counseling discoveries. She has shown a particular interest in women's sexuality and relationships, which perfectly complement my own. She is a member of

The Society for the Study of Sexuality and leads a women's therapy group. Consequently, the ideas that I was exploring with regards to intelligent lust were ones that we agreed she would experiment with, too.

While it may seem odd or even "creepy" for a father to engage his daughter in frank conversations about something as intimate as sex, I believe in treating the subject of sex with the same openness, honesty, and respect that I naturally would any other subject. As a therapist, friend, and father, I choose not to shroud sex in forms of secrecy and silence that foster dysfunctional and exploitative attitudes. My desire is to break down barriers and encourage healthy attitudes toward sex, acknowledge its value as a healing experience, and emphasize the meaning and satisfaction that smarter sex can bring to our lives.

As Alyssa learned to apply the steps of intelligent lust with her clients, we discovered that there were important gender and generational differences that influenced the particular direction of every case. As a result of our exchanges, my practice has been enriched by the perspective of a heterosexual female therapist of a significantly different generation who lives and works on the West Coast.

I have asked Alyssa to comment on the ideas and cases where appropriate throughout the pages of *Your Brain on Sex*, with the hope that her comments will enrich your experience, too.

NOTE ABOUT CONFIDENTIALITY
The identities of patients in this book have been carefully disguised in order to protect their privacy and the confidentiality of their therapy.

The Six Steps of Intelligent Lust

INTRODUCING
INTELLIGENT LUST

CHAPTER 1

How Sex Heals

> *"Healing may not be so much about getting better, as about letting go of everything that isn't you—all of the expectations, all of the beliefs—and becoming who you are."*
>
> —RACHEL NAOMI REMEN

The human body is designed to heal itself. We have an immune system that protects us from disease and repairs us when we are damaged. Pain acts as an alarm, alerting us to the problem. In response, all of the body's systems, including the mind, are called into action to aid in the process of self-recovery.

Similarly, when we encounter emotional conflict, we also experience pain. This can take the form of feelings of sadness, anxiety, fear, and anger, although sometimes it may manifest in the body through physical illness. The mind mobilizes its own defense to assist in repairing the emotional wound in the same way we release an army of antibodies to heal a cut finger. Whether it's physical or psychological, we are hard-wired to lessen pain, helped by innate mechanisms.

Among the mind's most inventive weapons in the battle for recovery and reconciliation are our fantasies. We create them to counteract anxiety or pain, substituting pleasure where conflict exists. We need only to spend time with a young child to remember what a central role fantasies have in our development as human beings. Children discover the world and themselves through fantasy play, mastering skills that they will use to face challenges throughout their lives.

In the rituals of fantasy play, children find comfort. They often return to the same fantasies, games, or objects again and again because their familiarity provides a zone in which they feel safe and increasingly competent. Children try out roles as sports stars, princesses, police officers, and superheroes, enabling themselves to feel powerful in a world in which grown-ups are in charge.

As we age and societal expectations and norms gradually restrict our imaginations and behavior, we shift from using play as a means to understanding and begin to apply the lessons learned toward navigating the harsher realities of adult life. Yet, we continue to use fantasies to help us gain mastery of challenging events. Now we imagine being billionaires or CEOs or celebrities, rewarded with power or fame for our accomplishments, or we fantasize writing the great American novel or producing a film, becoming the pillars of our community, or simply winning the lottery. We have learned to convert painful feelings of disappointment, powerlessness, failure, or loss into manageable and sometimes even pleasurable ones. This is the healing nature of fantasy, one of the mind's most effective mechanisms for coping with emotional crisis.

Like children's play and fantasy, sex exists as one of our greatest natural pleasures. Thinking back to the fun and freedom we experienced playing, we can draw a parallel with sexual play as adults.

During sex, we similarly enter into an ecstatic space in which we let go of all immediate worries and try out different roles. Like child's play, sex takes us to a level far from the mundane, a moment of exceptional intensity. Yet in sex, we take things even one step further. We use it to make our lives and relationships more vivid and robust.

Scientists agree that frequent sex can improve heart health, build a more robust immune system, and increase the ability to ward off pain. Sex changes brain and body chemistry, boosting certain hormone levels that keep us young and vibrant. Sex can also alter our mental state by releasing endorphins that act as antidotes to stress, anxiety, and depression. But among our greatest healing miracles is how we use sexual fantasies to work through deep-seated conflicts and satisfy unmet childhood needs.

By the time we leave adolescence, most of us have eroticized some aspect of these conflicts, encoding them in our sexual fantasies. The fantasies, which continue throughout our adult lives, transform the pain associated with old conflicts into pleasure.

As a society, we have a complicated relationship with sex, simultaneously promoting sexual images in popular culture—movies, television, and advertising—while demonizing those of us who enjoy it with labels like "whore," "slut," and "player." Sometimes sex is portrayed as a romantic seduction in which it's used to win the man. Other times partners are shown tearing each other's clothes off and engaging in ravenous behavior, giving the impressions that sex is primitive and instinctual and should require no thought. Many of us internalize these confusing or unrealistic messages. By the time we reach adulthood, we have no idea of what sex actually means to us personally. Nor do we have a sense of the healing effects sex can have in our lives as an experience in building trust, intimacy, acceptance, and authenticity. As a society, we have not yet discovered the deeper meaning of sex.

To avoid feelings of confusion or shame, we often attempt to suppress or erase our sexual desires and fantasies from our experience, if not from our consciousness altogether. This can result in a condition of alienation and inauthenticity—a disconnection between who we really are and how we behave. We enter a process of disengaging our minds from our bodies and souls, which often lasts a lifetime.

But the truth refuses to be buried. Denying our desires and fantasies ultimately does not work. The conflict will manifest itself in a wide range of sexual difficulties from the loss of sexual interest to feelings of dissociation in which we engage in sex but feel as if we aren't fully present. We feel numb, or imagine shopping at Saks or bowling a perfect score while we are "making love" with our partner. Other times our conflicts are reflected in our inability to orgasm, genital pain, or erectile dysfunction.

To help clarify the idea of the toll that repression can take, here's one of my cases—twenty-five-year-old Sam Watson, who came to therapy because he couldn't perform sexually on his wedding night.

TOO GOOD FOR HIS OWN GOOD: SAM

Unlike most young people today, Sam and his new bride, Erica, waited for their wedding night to consummate their marriage. But when it came time for sexual intercourse, Sam quickly lost his erection. When they were dating, they had regularly engaged in making out and petting, during which Sam always found himself aroused, but intercourse seemed to be a different matter entirely.

Sam was the eldest of five children raised by a single mother without the financial or emotional involvement of a father. Both his parents had emigrated from Ireland and met in New York at a church social, after which they never left each other's side. They married within a few months and had five children immediately, each two years apart. Their new family seemed to make up for the ones they left behind in Ireland.

A heavy smoker, Sam's father died of lung cancer after a protracted and painful illness. Sam was barely twelve at the time. Just before his death, Sam's father made Sam promise that he would take care of his mother after he was gone, a deathbed vow that Sam took very seriously.

Left with little money, Sam's mother worked hard as a housekeeper, taking care of the local church and a few of the larger homes in town. Sam's mother always managed her work and family responsibilities with grace, never issuing a complaint. She was admired by friends and neighbors, often held up as a model parent—hardworking, kind, and self-sacrificing.

Sam fulfilled his vow to his father by looking after the younger children. He helped them with homework, dressed, fed, and read to them daily. As he grew older, he took on more responsibilities, even accompanying his mother to parent/teacher conferences and church meetings. He often served as her companion. In high school he stayed close to home, never letting his mother down.

But this did not come without a price. At times, the responsibility felt too much for him. He wanted to join in the activities with other high school kids—play soccer, attend after-school clubs and school dances, but there was no time for that. And while he continued to measure up to his responsibilities, he secretly began to feel resentful.

By his senior year Sam had grown into a handsome boy. Girls teased and flirted with him, but he was too busy and too shy to date. He had discovered masturbation early—when he was barely a teenager—and had been enjoying it regularly ever since, despite the fact that he had been taught it was a mortal sin. By now he had begun to have regular sexual fantasies about some of the girls from school. With an edge of defiance, Sam took pleasure in secretly rebelling against the authority of the church, masturbating several times a day.

At some point toward the end of his senior year, Sam began to imagine having anal sex with girls, a fantasy that occurred occasionally at first but soon came to dominate his thoughts. His fantasies also grew increasingly aggressive over time.

When it was time for college, Sam stayed near home, attending the county community college so he could continue to look after his family. His fantasies about anal intercourse continued, yet he still had not experienced sex with a girl.

Then Sam met Erica. He felt lucky to have found a woman who was as kind, thoughtful, and hardworking as his mother. She shared a similar view of life and, like Sam, was a churchgoer who believed in the importance of close family ties. Erica was well liked by Sam's mother and siblings and easily fit into their family life. Soon they were all spending time together.

Sam was as respectful of Erica as he was of his mother, and while they were affectionate with each other, neither felt in a hurry to have sex. Kissing, holding hands, and light petting were enough for them. They had agreed to wait until they were married to have sex.

Privately, Sam kept up his fantasy life, which now had a second benefit. It helped him to maintain his abstinence with Erica.

Two years after they met, they had a big church wedding with more than two hundred people attending. But that's when the trouble started. As the wedding approached, the expectation of having sex with Erica weighed heavily in Sam's thoughts. He feared that he would not get excited by conventional sex and worried about maintaining an erection.

What he feared turned out to come true. "Missionary sex" did not arouse him, and he was unable to satisfy Erica or himself. He forced himself to keep his fantasies of anal sex out of his thoughts, banishing them while having sex with Erica. Where his fantasies once brought pleasure and relief, they now left him feeling inadequate and ashamed. So did his inability to perform. He grew irritable and frustrated, which soon extended beyond the bedroom. Because of their mutual shyness, he could not bring himself to talk with Erica about what he felt, and she, likewise, never raised the subject.

Finally, he visited his doctor but was too embarrassed to tell him the truth about his sexual desires. After a brief interview, the doctor diagnosed him with erectile dysfunction and prescribed Viagra.

But the Viagra didn't work, which sometimes happens when the underlying psychological reasons for a symptom are not dealt with. Sam still could not maintain an erection or reach an orgasm.

It wasn't until Sam entered therapy, at the suggestion of a forward-looking priest, that he began to understand that his inability to get or maintain an erection resulted from the disconnection between his true desires and the sex he felt he was expected to perform. Previously, he had not thought about the history and meaning of his desires and how well they actually served him or how much they were a part of a healing process. But by going through the initial steps of intelligent lust, Sam discovered that, without knowing it, he had eroticized his feelings of resentment. His fantasies of anal intercourse offered him an outlet for expressing his anger, allowing him a secret space to be a "bad boy" while dutifully fulfilling his vow of being a "good son" by continuing to act responsibly in his everyday life. Unfortunately, his guilt was strong enough to interfere with his inability to maintain an erection.

With my guidance Sam carefully initiated conversations about sex with Erica. He told her that he had been investigating his sexuality in therapy and that he now had some insight into his failure to be a better lover. At first, Erica didn't understand why Sam would share such private thoughts, or exactly what they meant. She had never had the benefit of therapy herself and was not naturally inclined toward making psychological connections. But Erica loved Sam and understood intuitively that Sam's pain was greater than her confusion. She worried about where the conversations might lead, but they had, so far, left her feeling closer to him. She asked him if he would mind if she went to therapy with him so she could understand him even better. Sam was delighted.

In our first session together, I explained to her the basic concepts of intelligent lust and why Sam and I had been discussing them. Although Erica confessed that sex was a mystery to her—"I never thought much about it"—she said she could appreciate the value of talking about it. "Even though it makes me a little nervous," she told me, "I already feel closer to Sam." Though not quite eager, she remained curious.

While I never directly asked her questions about sex, since we had agreed that our agenda was to "help her understand Sam," by the end of our second session she surprised us by volunteering to try following the steps of intelligent lust herself. Sam eagerly instructed her on the first step.

When they returned, Erica stated that, much to her surprise, she had "a kind of epiphany" while completing the first exercises. She realized that, like Sam, much of her life had gone into being the good girl and that despite her devotion to her parents and church, she secretly fantasized about what it would feel like to be "naughty." She recounted adolescent fantasies in which she imagined behaving like "a bad girl," sexually and otherwise, for which she remembered feeling guilty and ashamed.

Sam was excited to discover that his wife had spent as much time as him "thinking about what it would be like to be free. To be bad for a change. We were both way too good as kids."

In the next few sessions, Erica and Sam discussed the details of their fantasies and speculated on what they meant in relation to their past. And much to their relief, they discovered how complementary their sexual desires were. But when we discussed the ways they could act them out, Sam was the one who objected. He was not sure that he wanted to do this with the woman who was his wife. He worried that this would change his opinion of her, à la the Madonna/whore paradox. But Erica insisted she was game.

"For *God's* sake," she joked, "we need to have some fun. I'm not perfect. Definitely not like the Swan Queen in the ballet. I'm not going kill myself after you have your way with me." They both laughed. She said she strongly believed they could not only handle it but that "being naughty" would bring them even closer.

So with some nervousness and a lot of self-consciousness, they set out to follow the final step of intelligent lust by exploring their true sexual desires together. In the process they not only grew closer

to each other but also came closer to honoring all the complexities
of who they each truly are as human beings.

TAKING A STEP BEYOND INSIGHT

Does such insight make a difference? Is it enough to just understand our desires, or is it essential to the healing process to act out
our fantasies, regardless of their content?

Some psychotherapists, sexologists, and religious counselors
say emphatically no, we shouldn't, because enacting our fantasies
can reinforce and encourage the continuation of thoughts that
may then serve as a stepping-stone to pathological, antisocial, or
even violent behavior. According to this theory, a wide range of
sexual fantasies fit into this category because they fall outside of a
set standard of normalcy.

But what is normal exactly, and who determines it?

In actuality, definitions of "normal" are socially constructed,
continuously shifting over time as cultural attitudes change. Ho-
mosexuality, for example, once considered a perversion by mental
health professionals, was eliminated in 1973 as a psychiatric illness from the Manual of Diagnostic Categories. Other categories
of sexual "deviations" have similarly been dropped as our attitudes
toward sex have changed. For example, up until the eighteenth
century the age of sexual consent was twelve. In actuality, there
is no essential truth about what is normal, only what is socially
relevant at a given moment in time.

Additionally, there is no scientific evidence to support the no-
tion that acting out fantasies will lead to violent or perverse behavior the way drinking may lead to alcoholism. Regardless, some
of us believe we will feel worse for acting out a sexual fantasy—

perhaps even cheapened. "Dirty" thoughts should be kept secret, the thinking goes. But these feelings are more the result of the internalized shame and guilt we've been taught to associate with sex than they are decisions in support of self-respect or respect for our partners.

Our sexual desires reflect our unique histories and are as original and varied as we are as people. Far from random thoughts and feelings, they are healing instruments with meaning and purpose. By following the principles of intelligent lust, we can decode them and bring them to life safely and intelligently. If we can achieve authenticity by aligning our sexual behavior with our true desires, we can permanently change our relationships with ourselves and satisfy a host of deeper needs. Self-knowledge alone does not necessarily promote well-being; we need to use those insights and take action that breaks past patterns.

For centuries, philosophers have concerned themselves with the question of authenticity. Socrates may have been the first to state, "The unexamined life is not worth living," but it has been said innumerable times since.

For contemporary psychologists, a healthy and fulfilling life derives from the reconciliation between the external world and internal needs. Such authenticity requires knowing what those needs are and pursuing the goal of living them with honesty and integrity.

By challenging cultural values and norms, the steps of intelligent lust help us achieve the goal of authenticity. We arrive at our own set of moral values and obligations that derive from self-knowledge and self-acceptance.

Embracing our sexual truth reverses the corrosive influences of guilt and shame, and enhances the sense of self-worth and wholeness that is essential to leading a healthy life. We reclaim abandoned parts of ourselves and integrate them into our being, also crucial to health.

As we go through the process and gain insight, we also improve our relationships. No longer strangers to ourselves, we form relationships with greater sexual intimacy and compatibility. We connect with partners who understand our true desires and are willing to explore theirs as well. We continuously seek and exchange truths, a process that leads to a level of honesty beyond that normally achieved by partners and ultimately to a more satisfying relationship.

Through this journey we can accomplish something even deeper. We can counteract feelings of loneliness, powerlessness, inadequacy, and fear, satisfy unmet needs, and come to new terms with childhood conflicts. We reunite the mind, body, and soul in sexual experiences invoking the highest levels of our being. The journey itself is filled with mystery and beauty. It may be fast or unfold slowly with moments of pain and struggle. Yet, when we follow it, the realizations go deep and ultimately we find passion for life itself.

CHAPTER 2

A Case Study in Intelligent Lust

Emily's Story

Why is it that so many women reach their thirties frustrated and anxious about not having a life partner? The clock is ticking, and they feel a sense of urgency to marry and have children while they are still biologically able. They wonder how they got to this place—why no relationship has ever worked out.

And why is it that so many of us who do marry find ourselves in relationships in which sex has grown boring or has even disappeared after a relatively short time? We excuse its absence—"sex isn't that important; other things matter more. It's normal; everyone goes through it." Yet over time, resentment builds and feelings of rejection or disappointment quietly erode our sense of well-being.

The answer to these questions is simple—our lack of sexual intelligence. It's the main reason why so many relationships end in failure. It's why we make the wrong choices and why so many potentially successful relationships never begin. Instead, we base our choices on many factors other than sex, such as social standing, security, or similarity in backgrounds and religion. It's the rare couple whose sexual passion actually brings them to the altar, and when it does, it's too often because sex is "hot" rather than deeply meaningful and gratifying. Most of us either don't understand or ignore our true desires and consequently fail to use sex to guide us in choosing the best possible partner.

My patient Emily found herself exactly in this situation. When she began therapy, she had little awareness about how central sex was to her situation. She was confused about how to move forward in her life. She was in the "right" relationship yet felt stranded and alone.

By guiding Emily through the steps of intelligent lust, I helped her discover and use her true desires as a divining rod to find a partner not only with whom she was sexually compatible but also who helped her heal an old family wound.

My hope is that by reading Emily's story you will begin to consider sex in a new light. You will recognize how much sex has influenced your choices though, like Emily, without your awareness. You will also see that, by understanding the true nature of your sexuality, you can change the choices you make forever.

Don't worry about the absorbing details of the story or the specific steps. That will come later. Relax. Open your mind and let the meaning of Emily's story naturally find its way into your consciousness. It won't be long before you will use the steps of intelligent lust to help you make more meaningful and satisfying choices.

CHANGING THE COURSE OF FATE: EMILY

With her brown shoulder-length hair hanging neatly above her dark blue business suit, Emily sat in my office as though she were at work rather than at her first visit to a psychotherapist. A successful thirty-five-year-old event planner in Manhattan, Emily talked about herself easily but with little emotion.

Over the seven years since she had come to New York from Ohio, Emily had been fairly happy: she had a good career, a circle of kind friends, and she'd also had her fair share of dates, which hadn't amounted to much until she met Josh, a thirty-seven-year-old lawyer.

However, after a year of dating, Emily had put the relationship on hold. When I asked why, she said, "It had become boring."

When I then asked her to describe what she meant by boring, she told me the couple had fallen into a bland routine. Habits of Josh's that she once found endearing were getting on her nerves, and neither of them felt any thrill, although on paper they seemed a perfect match: Josh had an excellent job, a similar level of education, and the couple had many friends in common. But there was no magic.

While Emily's lack of interest in Josh was obvious in her words, I found the tense, unhappy expression on her face more revealing; it led me to ask, "What other feelings do you have besides boredom?"

Emily remained quiet for a moment. "I feel sad," she sighed. Her body relaxed somewhat.

"About what?"

"About Josh. That it's not working out."

I nodded. "Are you sad for yourself as well?" I asked.

"Yes, but it's more than just him. I just had my thirty-fifth birthday. And it was my scariest. I don't want to sound like a cliché, but it doesn't seem like there's much time left. The clock is ticking. I haven't made it work with anybody. I've never said this out loud, but I'm beginning to wonder if I ever will."

Her eyes began to well with tears.

At first I wondered if Emily experienced difficulty with commitment. But when I inquired about her other relationships, she told me of enduring friendships with women as well as men, and how she believed in sticking with her involvements. In fact, she said, if she had a problem, it might be that she often didn't know when to give up.

Despite her close friendships, she said she frequently felt lonely. "It's like a dull and steady ache," she said. "And it's going to get worse, I know it."

Her tears accumulated; I handed her a tissue and we sat quietly. As I suspected, behind the calm exterior ran deep currents of emotions, fear and sadness that she had been keeping from friends and, perhaps, herself.

Over the next week, when I thought about Emily, I wondered what other secrets she'd concealed and why she did so. It also struck me that, although she was attractive, Emily expressed almost no sexuality in her manner and appearance.

Early in the next session, I asked about Emily's sexual relationship with Josh. Patients often have difficulty discussing sex, and Emily wasn't an exception. She quickly challenged me, asking why the topic was important.

I told her that I was trying to examine all the possible sources for her difficulties with men so that we might find the best way to approach her dilemma.

She paused, frowned, and then admitted that she rarely spoke about sex, even with her girlfriends. When I asked why, she said that despite her liberal attitude toward sex in general, she found it "embarrassing" to discuss on a personal level.

I explained that most people would agree with her, but added that embarrassment is like any other feeling, and there's no better place to experience it than within the walls of the therapy room.

She decided to go ahead and talk about Josh—although she couldn't quite look at me as she spoke. She and Josh had never had "hot" sex, she admitted, and now they weren't having any sex at all.

When I asked why, Emily's face flushed. "No chemistry," she said. "Never, actually."

Emily was clearly uncomfortable, nervously shifting in her chair as she talked; she still refused to make eye contact. But over the years, I've learned that discomfort can yield substantial rewards, so I continued.

Emily told me about her conventional childhood in a Midwestern household. Her parents were teachers who recognized the importance of sex education in school, but as in so many families, sex was not discussed at home. And there were no signs that sex was a part of her parents' marriage.

I asked her how she was feeling right at that moment.

"I don't know," she answered. "Sex isn't easy to talk about. I try not to think about it. So I guess I'm anxious."

I asked her if she wanted to stop, because the questions I was about to ask were more challenging.

She shrugged. "I don't know," she said.

I've found that patients say "I don't know" when it's true. And also when it's not true. So I seldom pay attention to the words. Instead, I reassured Emily that she could stop the conversation at any time.

She nodded.

I then asked about her first sexual experience.

"You don't mess around," she said, and laughed. She explained that it was with a boy she'd dated during her freshman year in college, and the experience didn't amount to much. While at school, she never got serious about anyone, and although she often had sex with the men she dated, only once did she consider it "hot."

I registered this as important and planned to return to it, but for now, Emily was opening up and sharing information and I chose not to interrupt.

During her time in New York, she dated regularly but lost interest in men after a few months. While she occasionally had sex with these men, she never really enjoyed it. "Sex isn't that important to me," she said.

"Why is that?" I asked. She replied that she didn't have a strong sex drive.

When the conversation wound down, I returned to the information I'd noted earlier and asked her to describe the experience in college that she felt was hot.

Again, she looked away. "Even though it was a long time ago, I remember it really clearly. He had an amazing energy."

"What does that mean exactly?" I asked.

"He had this intensity about him—the way he moved, how he spoke, the way he paid attention to me. I was very attracted to him physically. Like I said before, that doesn't happen to me very often."

"What about his intensity was so attractive?"

She paused again. "I don't know. He exuded masculinity. I'm kind of ashamed to say that. I don't like those stereotypes, but most of the guys I meet aren't like that. They're just nice guys. Not that Ken wasn't nice, but he definitely had an edge. There was nothing boyish about him. He was visiting a friend of mine and we had sex a few times over the week that he was around."

I decided to take another chance and told her that I was about to ask some very personal questions, but that she would soon understand why.

She nodded slowly, which I took as permission to continue. I then asked her to describe with as much detail as possible her sexual relationship with Ken.

"He was very confident," she said. "He was in control from the start. He was aggressive, but not in an overwhelming way at first."

"What was your reaction to his aggressiveness?"

"I liked it. I feel funny saying this, but even though I didn't really know him, I wanted to let go with him. I just wanted to let him do whatever he wanted."

During the next few minutes, Emily described her memories of Ken. She seldom looked at me, focusing her eyes above my head and closing them slightly, like a cat focusing on some imperceptible object in the distance, as she recalled the best sex of her life.

"I liked that he dominated me. Even when I resisted, he'd have his way. That was a total turn-on. I enjoyed the feeling of submitting, being completely powerless with him. The last time we hooked up we spent all day in bed. I was really comfortable with him by then. It started slowly—a kiss on my neck, teasing my earlobe with the tip of his tongue. Then he made me strip for him while he sat and watched with his clothes on. He gave me instructions to do things to myself, to touch myself and get off in front of him. I'd never done that before. I don't even like looking at myself naked, but I really liked it. He would ask me to walk over to him, and he would make out with me. I would pull the zipper of his jeans down. Then he would abruptly push me away."

The more Emily talked, the more she became animated, her shyness turning into excitement. And she was looking right at me, as though the memory were making her brave.

"Eventually his instructions became more extreme. I felt like I was in a swoon. I know it doesn't sound romantic, but it was. After I proved that I would completely obey him, he rewarded me. He fondled me like I were a delicate piece of china. He made me come the first time with just the tenderness of his touch. The contrast with what had happened earlier thrilled me. Eventually we made love as sweetly and passionately as I ever could have imagined."

Suddenly self-conscious, she blushed a little. "I know this isn't exactly politically correct, but I loved the feeling of being power-less with him."

I thanked her for her openness and asked her if she was willing to be uncomfortable for just a little longer. "I have a question that might seem even more intimate."

She nodded her head and laughed. "Go ahead. I've come this far."

"I'd like to talk more about your fantasies. What do you think about when you masturbate?"

"Wow," she said, slightly stunned, and then she paused to think. "Well, I guess I don't masturbate much."

"Why?"

"Good question. I'm not sure that I want to keep going back to that place."

"Which place?"

"The place I went to with Ken—being submissive."

"But that is where you go then when you do masturbate?"

"Yes. I fantasize about what Ken and I did years ago. Sometimes I substitute other men I see on the street. But honestly, I don't mas-turbate very much."

"One more difficult question then we'll stop for today. What actually makes you climax? What thought or image do you have in your mind when you orgasm?"

She looked straight at me. "I don't think I've ever asked myself that."

"Ask yourself now," I said.

She hesitated. "It's more a feeling than an image."

"What's the feeling?"

"Total helplessness. Powerlessness."

I felt we were making good progress; we now had identified that Emily had unwittingly attached sexual pleasure to the desire to feel powerless—to be overwhelmed or dominated by a strong man.

But along with the pleasure came feelings of shame and guilt. Emily felt that by submitting in bed, she was in danger of compromising her identity as a strong woman. Unable to accept the paradox, she disowned her sexual desires and, in the process, grew increasingly alienated from her true self and from her partner. She repeatedly chose men who would protect her from this dilemma by never making her face it.

I wanted to understand more about the psychology of her situation, so over the next few sessions we talked about her relationship with her parents and siblings.

At first Emily described an average childhood. But when I asked about her relationship with her older brother, her mood turned sour. She sat up in her chair; her body stiffened defensively.

Her brother was the favored child, she said. "He could do no wrong. Both my parents adored him. He was a really talented athlete, like my father. Our lives were organized around practices, games, and going to sporting events. The television was always turned to the sports channels. I had no athletic talent and no interest in sports either."

Anger building, she paused to compose herself. I wanted to respect this awkward moment, but because I knew this was the time to explore her emotions, I asked Emily how her brother had treated her.

"He was totally selfish. I don't think either he, or my father for that matter, had any interest in me. I usually had to fight to get the family to do what I wanted, even something as simple as changing the channel."

"What was that like for you?"

"Not fun," she said.

"What did it feel like?"

Emily paused and then answered with a single word: "Powerless."

I sat silently. The word "powerless" had appeared again. We both recognized what she had said, but I left the word hanging in the air.

The connection between her feelings about her father and brother and her experience with other men was becoming evident. I wanted to place this in the context of sex, so in our next session, I began by talking about the many mysteries of desire. I told her that scientists understood very little about sexual attraction. Still, most psychologists agreed that sexual desire formed during early adolescence and solidified by young adulthood. Emily listened carefully.

"People's attractions are far more varied and original than anybody would like to admit. The details of these attractions are based on each person's unique psychology." I paused for a moment to gather my thoughts.

"As you noted last week, you felt powerless as a child because your father's and brother's interests dominated your daily life. We'll probably never understand the mechanism for exactly how this occurred, but somehow you eroticized that feeling of helplessness. I believe your true desire, the desire to be dominated, is your unconscious way of managing those feelings.

"This may be difficult to understand, but perhaps, by making the choice to be sexually dominated, even in your fantasies, you are turning the feeling of powerlessness that had brought you such great pain into something pleasurable."

Emily looked puzzled.

"I know this sounds paradoxical. But again, the experience of submitting to men—your brother and your father—is something you had no control over during your childhood, but, as a woman, by *choosing* to sexually submit—even if it's only in your fantasies— you symbolically gain control over those childhood feelings. By converting the pain into pleasure, you become the master of your powerlessness."

"Isn't that kind of, well, twisted?" Emily finally said.

"Not at all," I assured her. "The problem is not that you have these sexual desires. It's that you've never acknowledged and accepted them. Instead, it sounds like you disowned your sexuality and chose men who would not threaten you as your father and brother had. You stayed safe but at the expense of being bored with men and being unable to sustain a relationship with one."

"What do I do?" she asked.

"Many therapists," I said, "would spend years helping you work through those issues concerning your father and brother with the hope that you might eventually give up what they considered to be pathological, or at least immature, erotic desires. But I've come to believe that although such a strategy might prove helpful in resolving family issues, most people's true erotic desires will not necessarily change even after such a resolution."

I went on to say that I have found it much more helpful for people to understand the meaning and purpose of their true desires
and to honor rather than suppress them. I reminded Emily that
only once in her many relationships had she followed those desires
and that her brief affair with Ken was one of the most memorable
experiences of her life. Her relationships became boring because
she hadn't respected her true desires and instead chose men for
other reasons. By forbidding her physical attractions, she had sacrificed her core sexual identity.

"That formula has consistently failed," I said. "In fact, I believe
that you intuitively understood this was happening again with Josh—
which is why you chose to break off with him and enter therapy."

Now I took another leap, recommending that Emily experiment with dating men to whom she felt truly attracted and with
whom she might realize her fantasies.

"We've already established the importance of power in your
erotic life and that your true desire is to be dominated, which is
a perfectly reasonable and normal yearning. Now you just need
to learn how to use this knowledge to make better choices than
you've made in the past.

"I call this combination of sexual energy and self-awareness 'intelligent lust.' It's a powerful force."

"How does it work?" Emily asked.

"It's something I've been working on with a lot of my patients
for a while now."

"But lust? Doesn't that mean that I just marry the first guy I
lust after?"

"No, not at all. You don't want to be driven by lust alone. But
you also don't want to ignore your sexual drive. Either way, you're
giving up things that are important to you."

Emily nodded at this last sentence, knowing that she had made many poor choices over the years.

I continued. "Soon we can discuss how to use intelligent lust to guide your dating. But I don't want to get ahead of myself. What you need to do right now is figure out what qualities in men truly turn you on—the things that you feel make a man hot. And, of course, it's important to understand what those qualities represent.

"Let me give you an example. Let's say you feel attracted to men with short, thick bodies. When you stop to ask yourself why, the answer comes back that this type of body seems strong and powerful to you. Without even being aware of it, you conjure up feelings of submissiveness. Others who didn't eroticize power might not find these qualities a turn-on; they'd be attracted to different qualities.

"For you, just thinking this way will represent a pretty radical change, since rather than honoring your true desires in the past and choosing men with the qualities that turned you on, you denied them.

"Are you still with me?"

She nodded her head. "Yes," she said in a barely audible, but excited, whisper.

"Then let's take this next step. Between now and your next session, I'd like you to think about the qualities in men that most attract you, maybe even write them down. Think about chemistry. Try not to censor yourself. Let your mind roam freely. You're probably already aware of those qualities but have never sat down and actually thought them through."

The following week Emily's demeanor seemed lighter. She'd done her homework and generated a list of new discoveries. "Tall. Lean. Athletic body. Also, a rough beard, small tattoos, strong hands, and a distinctly cocky manner. And a certain smell, the natural kind a guy has after a long day."

None of the men she'd dated in the past possessed these qualities.

Now we talked about what the qualities symbolized. For Emily, a rough beard represented masculinity; a tattoo meant toughness; strong hands suggested power. This was the first time she had consciously thought about these attractions.

Emily was ready to move to the next step and discover what her fantasies meant. At the end of this session, I gave her more homework.

"I'd like you to think about all the details of your sexual fantasy. Ask yourself about the actual story surrounding the theme of domination and submission. Identify the action and the plot. What are you doing? What is your partner doing? What words are spoken? How do you feel? How does the fantasy end?"

I told her that if she had difficulty imagining the details, she could masturbate to conjure them up. She squirmed uncomfortably in her chair—a perfectly natural reaction.

In the next sessions, Emily reported, with mild embarrassment, that she had masturbated several times. The narrative in her fantasies remained constant: A man possessing her desired qualities convinced her to have sex during a long, intense conversation in which she challenged his cockiness, but ultimately surrendered. Sex started slowly, with gentle touching and kissing, but intensified as the man grew more persistent and demanding.

"Eventually," she said, "he'd get his way. I'd do anything he asked, like I was under his spell."

Now she became more animated, wanting to describe things in greater detail. "You asked me to think about how my fantasy ended. I figured out something that surprised me. I always ended up on top. I would make him come through my movements. Then I would have an orgasm too."

An interesting twist: In each fantasy she turned the tables and put herself in control of her partner's orgasm. I remarked, quite conscious of my wording, that it must be a *powerful* feeling to bring someone to climax in such fashion.

"Now that you understand this, it sounds like you're ready to replace the fantasy with real experiences," I added.

In the next sessions the topic was dating. We determined that Emily should be on the lookout for men with whom she felt chemistry based on the qualities she had identified. Now that she could allow it, sexual attraction would be her compass. She would be open to any man she met, regardless of his background. Most importantly she would stay open to her true desires as well.

Over the next six months, as we discussed other aspects of intelligent lust, I prepared Emily to apply the steps of intelligent lust to dating—in other words, to connect her fantasies to reality. Through coaching, she was becoming comfortable with the idea of acting them out. Emily dated frequently, each time becoming increasingly comfortable reading her sense of attraction. She let go of the artificial limits she'd created about similar backgrounds, ages, experience, and interests. With coaching, she talked about sex more easily. Men who seemed uncomfortable by the conversation did not make it to the next date.

"I feel empowered," she said. "I rarely get bored anymore. If I lose interest in a guy, I know why and I move on without wasting time. Chemistry isn't only about sex. It's also about enjoying differences and the tension they create. I've had some amazing fun with guys. I've gone on dates that would have been totally out of my comfort zone a year ago."

One evening, Emily and some friends went to a club to watch a rock band perform, and she was drawn to one of the musicians, Dan. He was stocky rather than lean, but he exuded masculine energy.

"He looked like a bit of a bad boy," she later told me. "The kind of guy I never would have let myself be interested in before."

Feeling confident, she stayed behind after her friends left and struck up a conversation. "We had a few drinks, flirted wildly, and exchanged phone numbers. He called the next day." Soon they were dating.

As she got to know Dan over the next several months, she learned that he was a native New Yorker who made his living as a physical trainer. "He's totally comfortable in his body and not at all shy about sex," Emily said. "I feel really comfortable with him. We had amazing chemistry from the start. We've already done a lot of sexual exploring. We're totally compatible. Best of all, I think I could fall in love with him."

When I inquired about the differences in their backgrounds, she said, "He loves that I'm a strong, successful woman. He has a lot of respect for me, and I do for him. He never tries to dominate me outside of the bedroom. In fact, we do a lot of what I want. I mean, it's not perfect. Stuff comes up. He hates that I work so late. He's not super-sophisticated. I don't like some of his friends and he doesn't like many of mine. But it works. We have so much going for us."

"What else do you have going for you other than what you already mentioned?" I asked.

Emily explained that in the process of exploring sex, the couple had developed a level of honesty, openness, and trust that Emily had never imagined possible. This fortified their bond and carried over into all aspects of their life together.

Emily had moved into the final stage in using intelligent lust, naturally, with little guidance from me.

"We talk about everything," she said. "I think that once we felt safe talking about sex, we weren't afraid to talk about anything. Isn't that the idea? To let yourself go? To take a risk and make yourself vulnerable even though you could be rejected—or wind up feeling like a fool?

"I think this makes us open about other emotions. Dan will come to me and tell me if I've hurt his feelings. And I know I can talk to him about whatever makes me feel insecure. If we can tell each other our wildest sexual thoughts—and even explore them— we can certainly support each other in whatever else we do in life. For the first time in my life, I really feel like myself.

"In the past, I'd hide my sexual feelings. How can you communicate and grow when you're hiding something that important?"

"It sounds like you've developed a strong sense of self-respect," I said.

"I think so," she said. "I know more about myself than I ever imagined—and I see who Dan really is in all his complexity. We know each other's good and bad and we still love and admire each other."

In six months I'll see Emily for a follow-up session. I don't know whether she and Dan will still be together. Life is unpredictable. But I do know that all human beings have an indomitable need for health and fulfillment, and Emily will be much closer to both.

ALYSSA'S THOUGHTS

As a thirty-five-year-old woman myself and a counselor who works primarily with women in their thirties, I find that Emily's case has particular relevance to me. In my experience it is often during this time in life that women seek out counseling, and it is, more often than not, due to dissatisfaction with their relationships and their sex lives. Emily was able to identify that the choices she was making in her life were not bringing her the results she wanted. She was beginning to internalize and interpret this dissatisfaction as some sort of character flaw, a fixed trait that most likely would cause a lifetime of loneliness.

In my experience, it is also not uncommon for women to attribute a sexual incompatibility to "low sex drive," though virtually all of them can describe times in their lives or partners with whom sex was frequent and satisfying.

Yet some part of Emily was able to recognize that perhaps an increased awareness in her underlying causes and motivations for her choices could help her change patterns, change the course of a fate she was hesitating to see as being sealed. That perhaps she could gain insight or learn a practice that could allow her to make decisions with more intention and consciousness. By dating men who "looked good on paper," Emily was only dipping her toe into the possible choices she had in partners. This is where many women are, a place that feels comfortably concrete. But by recognizing in herself only what was at the tip of the iceberg, she was missing information that held more substance.

Perhaps because I am a younger female practitioner, or perhaps because I live in Portland, a notably sex-positive and generally sexually permissive city, many clients who approach my services are comfortable talking about at least some aspects of sex. They typically have an idea of whom they are attracted to and what turns them on. Where I find most of my clients become stuck is in the process of translating their desires into action, the process of seeking out and finding appropriate partners and then in addressing their desires with them. The practice of assertiveness, or asking for what you want, is one that can be learned. Many women lack assertiveness skills, and there are many reasons for that, socialization and fear of rejection being at the top of the list. By first understanding the meaning of her desires, Emily was able to then translate insight into action, seeking out someone who was a better fit for her. She then expressed her desires in a way that showed integrity and confidence, despite the fact that it may have felt new and scary. This shift, the increased awareness and intentional action, makes it possible for many women to accept themselves and create relationships in all areas of their lives, both personally and professionally.

CHAPTER 3

A Closer Look at Intelligent Lust

"This is the body that engages in sex, a body with so much soul that any attempt to deny its layers of meaning will come back to haunt us."

—THOMAS MOORE

What is intelligent lust? We've been talking about it all along, so you are aware that it is a process in which we discover our true sexual desires. By that I mean we bravely explore what really turns us on and then begin to think about where those desires come from and what they mean. Then, perhaps the most challenging but exciting part, we use those insights to create a meaningful, satisfying, and healing sexual life.

Lust (the craving for sexual pleasure) can best be described as selfish—our passion for the object of sexual interest is placed above all reason. It is empty, mechanical, and soulless. Examples of lust are plentiful in all forms of meaningless sex such as random anonymous sex or sex under the influence of alcohol or drugs.

Intelligent lust, on the other hand, engages the body, mind, and spirit to give and receive physical pleasure through a deep emotional connection to ourselves and another. It is a process that involves searching for authenticity, unity, and purpose beyond the simple desire for sexual gratification. It is the source of deep satisfaction and beauty, though unsentimental and sometimes ruthless.

The steps of intelligent lust foster

- *In the body*: The biological urge for physical pleasure and gratification. The full engagement of our bodies as an erotic landscape.
- *In the mind*: An understanding of and respect for our desires, where they come from, and what they mean. Self-acceptance: a consciousness of our worth. The engagement of our imagination and intuition.
- *In the spirit*: Respect and generosity toward ourselves and partner. The desire to achieve a higher purpose through the deep engagement of sex. An open heart from which to heal ourselves and our partner.

The steps of intelligent lust begin with discovering our authentic sexual needs and desires. We organize a bundle of confusing thoughts and fantasies into a clear definition of our sexual truth. We embrace the reality of the facts rather than denying them.

For the most part, this is a solitary process. But once we are stripped of our veils and masks, the our goal with intelligent lust is to transform self-knowledge and self-acceptance into action. We accomplish this by manifesting new sexual experiences that are authentic, meaningful, and restorative in nature.

TRANSFERENCE

At some point during the course of most intimate relationships, we project onto our partner feelings and expectations that originated in our own childhood experiences. Often we choose a significant other with qualities similar to a parent with whom we experienced conflict, essentially finding a new edition of an old relationship. In our desire for reconciliation and catharsis, we create an emotional warp in which we drag the past into the present by reenacting the old conflict with our new partner, this time hoping for a different outcome in which our partner gratifies our needs and makes whole what was fractured or incomplete. But because we chose a partner based on our projections, he or she cannot make us whole and we go deeper into our loneliness and despair. Psychoanalysts call this process *transference*.

My patients Jenny and Mark had a marriage that fell victim to the effects of transference.

When Jenny met Mark, she was instantly attracted to him. Both originally Midwesterners, they came from a similar family and religious background, and both were college educated. Mark ran a successful insurance business in the suburbs of New York; Jenny was a fourth-grade teacher in the same community. She admired his family values and solid work ethic, which were much the same as her own. Socially, he was gregarious in contrast to her shyness, which she felt complemented her perfectly. He seemed level-headed and decisive, much the way her father had been. They fit easily into each other's lives, enjoying a sense of familiarity and easy comfort.

While Jenny felt she had a good childhood, she never believed she was able to command her father's full attention. No matter how she tried—getting good grades, dressing pretty, or acting defiantly—

Jenny could never get him as interested in her as he was in her brothers, both stars of their high school varsity baseball team. Since her father had played baseball in college, but fallen shy of a professional career, he had his hopes pinned on his sons. He clearly favored them.

Although Mark was like her father in many ways, he was different in one important way. She had never experienced such warmth and affection. It more than made up for what she missed from her father. She glowed in its flame. And their sexual relationships were "hot." Jenny could seduce Mark at the drop of a hat. She enjoyed teasing him, rewarding him with sex, and setting up surprise sexual adventures. Where she had failed at getting her father's attention as a child, she could succeed with Mark by using sex. She even got him to pay her for it with expensive gifts. She felt powerful. She was sure that the attention Mark showed her during their courtship would continue far into the marriage. But she was wrong.

With the responsibilities of new marriage in mind, Mark felt an obligation to earn money for his and Jenny's future. He began to put longer hours in at work and at home was always working at his computer. He felt secure in the marriage and that the best way he could show his love for Jenny was to protect their financial future. After all, she wanted a beautiful home, children, and a comfortable social life.

On the weekends he started to play ball with his friends and office mates in order to "blow off steam." And while Jenny was always invited to come along and watch, she increasingly preferred to stay at home. "He works hard," she thought. "He deserves to have fun."

Before she understood exactly what was happening, she found herself in the same position she had been in as a child, "craving a man's attention." She continued to flirt with Mark, buying and dressing in sexy clothes, but she usually failed to get his attention. He was tired or distracted. He was busy building his business and hanging out with the guys. Soon her marriage completely echoed her childhood. They began to argue about other issues like household responsibilities and spending money. Jenny became depressed.

The same feelings of failure and inadequacy that she had experienced as a child now dominated her marriage. While she had chosen Mark because he had many of her father's "best qualities," she had also unconsciously *transferred* on to him the expectation that he would satisfy her unmet childhood needs, making up for the lack of her father's attention. And without her awareness, she had eroticized the conflict, imagining that by using sex as a tool to gain Mark's attention, she could solve it.

THE RESTORATIVE EXPERIENCE

What if we set out instead to consciously identify our true sexual desires and the underlying conflict from which they sprang? Well, if we understand the nature of our desires, they will tell us what is needed and what is best. We could specifically choose a partner with whom we are deeply sexual and otherwise compatible, and who has the qualities that can enable us to heal from those unresolved feelings for which our true desires act as antidotes.

By following the steps of intelligent lust, we create a *restorative experience*, based on intimacy, respect, trust, and honesty, that can have a profound emotional and spiritual effect on us, whether it's in the context of a brief encounter or ongoing relationship. We give preference to self-awareness, exploration, and authenticity over sexual performance or reaching an orgasm.

In a restorative experience, we create a safe and consensual encounter in which we act out with our partner a fantasy we have imagined in our fantasy life and whose symbolic meaning we have already come to understand.

Whether the scenario is as conventional as romantic seduction, or as unusual as extreme bondage fantasies, we connect—physically, emotionally, and spiritually—with the deepest part of our psyches, recovering what was suppressed or lost. In the process, we restore ourselves to wholeness.

Of course, the deepest and most lasting healing comes when we have the opportunity to experience our true desires and work through the mastery of the conflicts behind them over time. Whether it's with a lover or spouse, a *restorative relationship* assumes an emotional posture that is often diametrically opposite from the dysfunctional ones we experienced in our childhood. Characterized by openness, intimacy, and mutual respect, the new relationship allows us to derive a new settlement to old conflicts. Within this friendship, sex is not separated from the joys and struggles of daily life, nor diminished by its challenges. Instead it offers a rich and fertile ground for a meaningful and satisfying life.

Mark and Jenny had the seeds of a restorative relationship from the beginning of their courtship. Mark had some of Jenny's father's "best qualities" and many of his own. But sadly, over time, he came to favor her father's worst behavior: withdrawing his attention. This eventually left Jenny feeling lonely and isolated, similar to how she had felt when she was growing up.

Why did this happen?

Mark had been raised in a family always on the edge of financial disaster. As the "sensible son," he saw it as his duty as a young man to support his family. Now, as a married man, he wanted to do whatever possible so that he and Jenny never suffered similar financial concerns. As much as Jenny resented Mark's increasing absence from family life, Mark secretly resented the burden of what he felt was his responsibility. Jenny, however, never actually expected him to shoulder this responsibility alone—it was he who expected it from himself. Without being aware, Mark had transferred unresolved feelings of anger and resentment toward his family of origin onto Jenny. Further, where Jenny had eroticized the rejection she felt in her family, using sex as a tool to win Mark's attention, Mark had turned his resentment into sexual withdrawal. He even masturbated while thinking about disciplining Jenny for expecting too much from him.

Since neither Mark nor Jenny consciously understood the transference in which they enacted their daily interactions, they gradually drifted from the warmth and affection that initially characterized their relationship. Not surprisingly, they each found themselves feeling similar to the way they felt in their own families—the very feelings they had hoped to escape by marrying. It was only after following the steps of intelligent lust that Mark and Jenny realized they could use what they had each eroticized to turn their relationship around.

Understanding how they had each sexualized their family conflicts began to mend the emotional and sexual distance that had come to divide them, but such insight wasn't enough to create real change. With my guidance, Mark and Jenny began to plan sexual encounters in which they acted out their fantasies and secret desires. They played out scenes in which Jenny deliberately used sex to bargain for Mark's attention; she traded sex, the kind Mark liked, for other time together. Mark enjoyed disciplining Jenny, which required a level of attentiveness that Mark had never given before. It was as much the honesty and intimacy achieved in their planning sex, as the gratification they came to mutually experience through it, that helped them restore the elements of their relationship that had originally attracted them. That is, they found again the attentiveness that once seemed so abundant to Jenny and the feelings of trust and security that made up for the absence of it in Mark's family of origin. By following the steps of intelligent lust, Mark and Jenny were able to use sex to reverse the corrosive effects of anger, resentment, and disaffection, opening the door to a better future together.

Similarly, by following the steps of intelligent lust, my patient Jason finally broke through a long-standing pattern of failing relationships, generated by issues of transference, to cultivate a restorative one that nourished his deepest desire for sensuality and affection.

REVERSING TIME: JASON

Nearly two years after his divorce, Jason came to see me for a consultation. Forty-five, tall, and handsome with deep blue eyes and a shock of gray hair, Jason was having problems with women. He had no trouble meeting them, but he found that after dating for a few months, they would invariably end the relationship.

When I asked him why, he said, "Women think I'm too laid-back. I get called things like passive or dull. They lose their patience or get bored. They yawn in my face."

By the time he'd come to see me, Jason had given up dating and was spending his free time in his workshop repairing old watches, avoiding the world. But a good friend confronted Jason, who confessed he was deeply depressed over his relationships with women; the friend encouraged him to seek therapy.

Shy and soft-spoken, Jason grew up in a privileged New England family with a long history of inherited wealth and a short history of accomplishments. Although Jason's father was an architect, he had never achieved much success nor had he cared. Instead, he enjoyed time on the golf course at the same club to which his own father and grandfather had belonged.

Jason informed me early on that he was "proud to be a terrible disappointment" to his parents. When I asked him how he'd disappointed them, he replied, "Because I refused to follow the social agenda they set for me."

Instead, he had devoted himself to more intellectual pursuits like reading and writing poetry, and watch repair—he even owned a small repair shop. When he wasn't being "totally ignored by his father," Jason said, he was being berated by him for his disloyalty to family tradition, a label Jason wore like a badge. Jason's mother, whom he described as "cold," put most of her energy into fundraising for local charities. "Everything for strangers, nothing for family," Jason said.

Although Jason told me that he'd rejected his family's social expectations, he nonetheless found himself dating women from his same social class. "In general," he said, "they turned out to be more like my parents than not. And mostly they choose me."

While it seemed obvious that Jason's depression was related to his long-standing conflict with his parents, I chose to approach it by first examining his failure with women, the symptom that had brought him to therapy.

When we began to talk about chemistry, Jason seemed puzzled by the concept. "It's not something that's ever happened on my end," he said. When I asked why, he insisted he had no idea. When finally pushed to explore what might attract him, he imagined a woman with "a kind, open face, delicate features, and a sweet disposition" adding, "nothing like the women I've gone out with." This seemed to come as a surprise.

As the therapy unfolded and Jason grew more comfortable exploring his sexual fantasies, he came to understand that what actually aroused him was the image of being gently caressed. He craved tenderness—"soft kisses and gentle fondling." In the past, when he engaged in sex with women, his orgasms came prematurely or not at all, disappointing everyone. Now, when he brought himself to orgasm, he imagined "the gentle touch of fingers brushing against my back." Jason soon recognized that he had unknowingly sexualized the qualities that he had so long ago craved from his parents—warmth and tenderness.

It was clear now how his lack of authenticity had contributed to his failures. In his past sexual practice, he had never experienced such feelings because the women who had chosen him were cold, no match for what he now recognized as his true desires. Caught up in his rebellion against his parents, he had sabotaged his chance at happiness by engaging with women who resembled them and whom he would then punish by withdrawing until they gave up.

Once Jason understood this, he decided he could break the cycle and search for an experience in which he could honor his true sexual desires. For the first time, he felt excited about dating. He posted a profile on a popular Internet dating site that included brief and poetic descriptions of his sexual interests and within a short time received a dozen well-suited responses.

Within a few months Jason had met a woman whom he described as "lovely." And as shy as he was, Jason took my advice and began to talk about sex after a handful of dates. He opened the conversation by speaking about his own experiences, and then gently working toward asking about hers. By then the conversation seemed natural. They quickly discovered that they felt the same way about sex—they were both turned on by gentle touching and tenderness. It wasn't long before they were having sex.

"This was the first time I actually made love," Jason told me, "and it was tender and beautiful. I find myself wanting to be generous with her in every way and for hours. She asks nothing of me, expects nothing from me. She comes from a middle-class family, the sort my parents wouldn't have talked to. But I've met them also, and they're as kind as she is. I've finally realized that being in a family doesn't have to mean being in a prison."

Jason had broken the cycle. By following the steps of intelligent lust, he discovered his true sexual nature then succeeded at choosing a partner not only with whom he was sexually compatible, but also who enabled him to heal an old family conflict.

• • •

In following the steps of intelligent lust, we cultivate a life in which sex serves as the pathway for understanding some of the profound mysteries of our existence. We go to the trouble of making sex an art that fully engages body, mind, and spirit and gives us depth and humanity. And while we live from a place of meaning and purpose, we make pleasure a priority.

Without the benefit of intelligent lust, we wander through relationships, confused to why they feel unsatisfying or repeatedly fail. Detached from our true selves, we are more likely to suffer from sexual addictions or romantic obsessions or show signs of performance anxiety, lack of interest, and other sexual dysfunctions, or we may act on lust impulsively or recklessly. Without self-knowledge and self-acceptance, we cannot bring complexity to our imaginations and therefore no real resolution to the emptiness and boredom that fill our relationships.

ALYSSA'S THOUGHTS
Feeling Accepted

It seems to me as if something that virtually every human being is looking for is the feeling of being accepted for who we truly are. And if we are ever to achieve such a thing, it cannot be done without first acknowledging and accepting ourselves. We then must find the courage to share this. With sharing, with any connection to any other person in fact, comes risk. For we cannot control them or predict the outcome of each inherently unique connection. It is in our willingness to risk that that we bare our soul.

In a society that glorifies individual power and success, it's easy to lose sight of the satisfaction we can feel by being generous to others. There is, in my opinion, very little that feels as good as giving openly and without expectation, not only the kind of giving that comes from sharing who we truly are, but also giving pleasure to another person. Seeing your partner for who he or she is and listening without judgment to what he or she likes facilitates his or her growth as well as your own. Embodying a spirit of giving and compassion can leave you content in a much more permanent way than any temporary receiving of pleasure can bring. Furthermore, being permitted to participate in someone's deepest longings can create an intense bond based on mutual respect and, of course, acceptance. This is how sex heals the soul.

Step 1: Getting in the Right Frame of Mind

Opening Up to Your Sexuality

"To find yourself, think for yourself."

—SOCRATES

Following the steps of intelligent lust requires creating the time and space for quiet contemplation as well as finding the same presence of mind and commitment that we would bring to therapy. Before we begin, there are things we can do to help get us in that right state of mind.

In the practice of psychotherapy, the consultation room plays as important a role as the conversation that occurs within its borders. It guarantees the patient a safe, neutral space for thoughts and feelings to be untangled, experienced, and expressed. Its walls delineate a boundary within which the focus is solely on the patient without any distractions or interruptions. The room creates a womb-like feeling that satisfies a deep primal need in us. In it, thoughts and feelings can grow, be confined, or kept secret. Things can be discussed in this room that cannot be approached anywhere else.

Finding a space free of distractions, equivalent to the privacy and purpose of a therapy room, improves our sense of comfort and safety as we open our minds to following the steps of intelligent lust. A neutral place, absent of personal history, prevents contaminating the experience with negative associations or memories. It's where we can think out loud all that we have grown accustomed to keeping silent, in the hope that we might understand ourselves and come to terms with our desires.

Designate a place to use—a garden, park bench, beach, backyard deck, front porch, or even the back seat of a car—to navigate the exercises. Keep a notebook or diary handy to record your experience. As you make progress, some exercises will require a completely private place away from public spaces. Scout one out before you begin.

1. TRUST IN YOUR TRUE DESIRES

Most of us have some sense of what turns us on, though we may not have put it into words or actual images. We know the kinds of experiences that excite us—the type of bodies that attract us, what style of kissing arouses us, where we like to be touched. But few of us know why we have chosen these preferences and how elegantly they serve us.

Have faith in the healing power of your desires. Keep this mantra in mind. *Our fantasies are antidotes that have meaning and purpose.* Whether it's a wish to be dominated like Emily, or to be tenderly made love to like Jason, our sexual fantasies convert painful, confusing, or unresolved feelings from the past into manageable and pleasurable ones in the present. We use them to transform helplessness into power, loneliness into emotional attachment, inadequacy into competence, weakness into strength. If properly understood, we can use them to find energy and direction to reconcile old conflicts and satisfy unfulfilled needs. Honor them as you would a friend.

2. GIVE YOURSELF PERMISSION TO EXPLORE

All our lives we have been learning about sex. Our earliest experiences as children inform us about intimacy, trust, gender, and power. Much of this we learn by observing how our parents treated each other as well as how we ourselves were treated. Some of us grew up with parents who acted as if sex didn't exist, ignoring our childhood questions and curiosities as if it were better not to think about sex. Others had parents who didn't feel good about themselves sexually. We read in their attitudes signs of fear, shame, or disgust. All of these experiences shape our feelings about what is responsible, right, or appropriate sexually, sometimes leading to some pretty rigid definitions.

The process of exploring sex should fall within the normal developmental struggle to define ourselves as we move from adolescence into adulthood. But because sex is considered so taboo, only in those rare families in which we are openly encouraged to consider it do we engage in what should be a healthy investigation.

In many families, the indoctrination into the "correct" way to think about sex can be so subtle and alienating that we never examine what is actually true for ourselves. Instead, our attitude toward sex is based on what we are taught and how we are expected to behave around it.

Yet even experts vary on what a definition of healthy sex should be. Why should we then accept someone else's ideas about sex before we identify and understand our own desires and ideals? Instead we should dig deep into our souls and psyches and examine what we truly feel about sex even at the risk of feeling disloyal to our families or churches like Erica and Sam. Following the steps of intelligent lust requires giving ourselves permission to be different.

3. BE COMPASSIONATE TOWARD YOURSELF

Compassion is the ability to feel another person's distress along with the desire to relieve it. We learn about it when our parents show their deep concern toward us during moments of upset or pain, validating our feelings by reflecting them back to us in words. We also observe it in how our parents behave toward each another as well as toward themselves. If our parents act with kindness and gentleness during times of upset, we will eventually come to internalize that modeling, and compassion will become part of our emotional repertoire.

If in the process of identifying our sexual desires, we discover that our most powerful fantasies are in conflict with our self-image, this conflict may lead to feeling confused and distressed. A patient who is the CEO of a large corporation, for instance, had great difficulty reconciling his role as leader with the fact that he desired to be dominated in bed. His discovery initially led to feelings of embarrassment and shame.

When such surprises occur, we must suspend all self-judgments, tone down the moralism, draw from our reservoir of compassion, and direct it toward ourselves. Life is full of contradictions and paradoxes, which, with maturity, we learn to accept. To become whole we must fully embrace and integrate all parts of ourselves and our desires, however contradictory, dark, or difficult they may appear.

4. CONFRONT THE CONSEQUENCES OF CHANGE

All change has its consequences. But sometimes the price of change seems greater than the cost of remaining the same. When it comes to sex, it may feel safer to maintain the status quo than to delve too deeply into our thoughts and fantasies for fear of what we might discover about ourselves or what others might find out about us. If our desires stray too much from convention, we imagine the worst: We will be punished for our "sins," attacked for our "selfishness," or labeled crazy for our "kinkiness." We may even preempt others from criticizing us by diminishing ourselves first, a process that lowers self-esteem.

Instead, we can choose to act courageously, acknowledge the discomfort that comes with change, and still move forward. By confronting our fears, we have the potential to discover not only many truths about ourselves, our relationships, and our partners, but also a passion for life itself.

5. COMMIT TO MAINTAINING OPENNESS AND ACCEPTANCE

The first four steps of intelligent lust should be done independently even if we are in a committed relationship and our partner is also reading this book. We need the privacy to sort through what we really feel, think, and believe in relation to sex before we share our discoveries. There are often vagaries to our thoughts at first. It may take time for them to solidify and for us to feel certain and secure with what we believe is true. It's best to not share prematurely and wait until we reach step 5 to initiate that process. You will find instructions for engaging in such conversations in that chapter.

Still, following the steps of intelligent lust together will require a commitment from both parties to maintain openness, honesty, and acceptance regardless of the outcome. That you must agree to from the start. Acknowledging our most intimate desires to ourselves is difficult enough, but disclosing them to a partner can be terrifying. If, over a period of time, a partner has experienced us in a particular way sexually, new revelations can elicit reactions ranging from excitement to horror. A patient whose husband described her as sexually uptight revealed to him in therapy that she had a secret desire to dress and act like a slut. He told her the idea was extremely sexually arousing. But in a similar case, a wife's fantasy of wearing sexy lingerie instead aroused her husband's disgust and, as a result, her own shame and embarrassment.

Hearing about a partner's fantasies when it involves a third person can feel especially threatening and in some cases torturous. Feelings of jealousy, betrayal, or suspicion generally grow out of deeper feelings of inadequacy in which we fear that we're not interesting or sexy enough to hold the attention of a partner.

But as we begin to understand our partner's relationship and family history and its connection to their desires, most of us develop a more generous perspective. We find value in building a truthful, trusting, and authentic relationship as a replacement for feelings of inadequacy, jealousy, and insecurity and recognize the extraordinary gift of being invited into our partner's inner world and sharing in its many truths.

6. ACCEPT AND HONOR YOUR TRUE DESIRES

Our fantasies and desires remain relatively constant throughout our lives because the unmet needs from which they originate

often go unsatisfied or the underlying conflicts remain unresolved. Many women focus their sexual attention on the desires
of their partners and simply don't know or place value on their
own. Satisfying them is random and infrequent. If we treat our
desires as secondary, suppressing, denying, or holding them as
secret, they will influence us in subversive ways, possibly manifesting in illness, addictions, depression, acting out, and other
negative symptoms.

By accepting and honoring our true desires, we take responsibility for their gratification and create the opportunity for them to
truly serve their healing purpose.

IT'S NOT SO BLACK AND WHITE: LEON

When Leon was just a toddler, his father was recruited to head the
engineering division of a large auto manufacturer. The family left
the small Louisiana town where their roots went back generations
and headed to the suburbs of Detroit, the flourishing automobile
capital of America. Leon's mother quickly found a job as a high
school social studies teacher for which she had trained at Louisiana
State University. It was an exciting change for his parents, but for
Leon, who was wrenched from the arms of his loving grandmother
who looked after him every day while his parents worked, it was a
profoundly difficult adjustment. When they arrived in Detroit, the
family immediately began their jobs and Leon was left in the care
of Lucy, a Jamaican nanny, whose employment was arranged by
the auto company. Much to his parents' surprise and delight, Leon
bonded with his new caretaker, who was gifted with kindness and
warmth. She embraced Leon as if he were her own, providing him
daily love and affection as his grandmother had.

Lucy remained with the family after Leon entered school. When his sister Jean arrived, Lucy took care of her as well. Over time, she became integrated into family life, participating in nearly everything they did as if she were a family member. Feelings of warmth and affection were shared by everyone. Still, to those outside the family she was considered the "help," and more than a few tongues wagged about how close the "negro girl" was to family. "It isn't good for the children," they said. "They should take care of their own." At the time there were strong racial tensions in Detroit, particularly in the auto industry, where the highest-level executives like Leon's father tended to be white when most on the assembly lines were African American. But everyone in the family, including Lucy, was happy and doing well, so it was easy for them all to turn a blind eye to the social criticism.

When Leon was fourteen, the family's bliss came to a tragic end. On the way home from the company Christmas party, a drunk driver lost control of his car, crossed the highway divider, and hit their car head-on. Leon's parents died instantly.

Upon hearing the news, the extended family acted urgently. Worried about the children, the relatives made the decision to bring them back to Louisiana to live with their grandmother.

After the funeral, Leon and his sister were quickly gathered up and sent south. Perhaps because family members didn't know how close Lucy and the children had grown, or maybe as a result of Southern prejudice, Leon and his sister were not given the opportunity to say good-bye to Lucy.

Leon had a very difficult time adjusting to life back in the South. He was grieving not only the loss of his parents, but also the loss of his beloved Lucy. Already a shy teenager, he withdrew further into the solitary world of books, and despite his grandmother's many attempts to encourage Leon to participate socially with friends and family, he remained "a loner" throughout his remaining teenage years.

When Leon came to see me shortly after his thirty-fifth birthday, his grandmother had recently died. He subsequently had spiraled into a depression from which he could not find his way out. We spent several months talking about his past, reliving his life before and after the tragedy, his feelings about his grandmother, his parents, and, of course, Lucy. Within the safety of my consultation room, Leon gradually allowed himself to grieve. When he finally let go, it seemed as if his tears would never end. But at last they did. He wrote to Lucy, whom he learned now had her own children. They began a warm correspondence.

After his major depression lifted, Leon raised another concern. He was forty and had never had a substantial relationship with a woman. While he understood now that he had been depressed since adolescence and that his depression had influenced all of his relationships, he had become comfortable enough with me to reveal a secret he had kept hidden from everyone.

Confused and ashamed, his head bowed when he spoke, Leon told me that he compulsively fantasized about sexual relations with "black girls." When I asked him specifically what he meant, he said, "The only time I can get off is thinking about having sex with a black woman and I am her master. I have been thinking about this for as long as I can remember."

I asked him why he thought that was a problem.

"It's the whole white master thing. It feels wrong. It just doesn't seem right. I know somehow the whole sordid thing is related to Lucy. How couldn't it be? She was probably the most important person in my childhood. It feels totally creepy."

I asked him if it was Lucy he imagined in his fantasies.

"Hell no," he said, "but it's close enough. I've tried to make myself stop thinking about black girls, but I can't stop the thoughts. It feels like an obsession, the more I try not to think about it, the more I do."

"What do you actually feel?" I asked.

"I'm ashamed. I'm trying not to think of it as incestuous. But Lucy was a mother-figure. And beyond that—the whole white/black thing is nuts. I grew up in the South where there was a black/white fetish. It's just wrong!" he said again. "I'm disgusted with myself. When I do have sex with black women, I feel guilty and ashamed after. But I am just not into white girls—no attraction at all. I'm sure that's why I've never had a relationship."

His feelings seemed so intense that I felt before I could guide him through the steps of intelligent lust, which I believed would enormously benefit him, I would have to help him get in the right state of mind—to get him ready for the emotional journey and what he might discover. He said he felt as if his fetish loomed as large as his grief did.

I explained that for many years he had been quietly mourning, which left little energy or inclination for much else. His work had provided some distraction and relief from the droning of his grief, but it kept him isolated. I told him now that he was feeling less depressed, our goal in therapy would be to understand what motivated his desires and how he could use them to feel more satisfied in his life both sexually and otherwise—perhaps even heal old wounds. I suggested we build his interest and energy back slowly.

Before we began, I recommended that he choose a quiet place, free of any distractions, that he could use to engage in conversation with himself, journal writing, and quiet contemplation. He had

come to New York to further his career as a computer program-
mer, making his home in a small suburb just outside the city on
Long Island, where he had, by then, grown to feel quite comfortable. He chose the public library of this town as his private space
in which to do the exercises. He explained that he had spent many
fond hours in libraries during his childhood: "They allowed me
the solitude and solace I needed."

I asked him to start his journal by writing all the reasons that
he felt ashamed or guilty of his sexual desires. I suggested he push
himself to think of at least five. Start each sentence with, "I feel
ashamed or guilty about..." When he finished, I recommended he
re-read what he wrote twice and then, at the top of the list, title it
with the statement, "Self-Defeating Thoughts." I further suggested
that he refer to the list frequently when we later followed through
the steps.

When he returned, he read the list to me. It included, "I feel
guilty about being a racist. I am ashamed that I am out of control of
my thoughts and feelings. I feel guilty that I'm not sexually attracted to white women. I feel guilty about being disloyal to my white
Southern family for being attracted to black girls. I feel ashamed
that I treat black women as sexual objects."

We talked in depth about his guilt and shame over the next
few sessions, particularly about his disloyalty to his "white" family. I reminded him that his fetish, like all desires, had a specific meaning and purpose, and that we would soon discover
the true significance when we embarked on the next few steps
of intelligent lust. I asked him to think of his attraction as an act
of loyalty to his parents, rather than betrayal. When he looked
confused, I explained.

"Your parents didn't share the prejudices that other members of your 'white' family and community may have harbored. As you told me yourself, they fully embraced Lucy and she them. They came to love and trust each other despite the racial barriers that prevailed at the time." I further explained that regardless of their middle-class existence, his parents were unconventional in their values and that real loyalty to them would mean following in their footsteps. I suggested that he return to his favorite place in the library and write on the next page of his notebook the following mantra:

"I am willing to break convention and explore my personal truth."

I suggested he could best honor his parents by giving himself permission to be different. To be himself as his parents had done. I told him to re-read this sentence regularly over the course of the week. I further recommended that he practice acting more compassionately toward himself by trying to not judge himself or imagine how others would judge him. "Moralism gets in the way of discovering the truth," I added.

In the next session, Leon told me he was feeling more relaxed. He said that although he still didn't understand the reason for his preference, he did feel a little less guilty about having it. He had even masturbated without trying to stop his thoughts and concluded, for the first time, without feeling ashamed.

I told him this was an important sign—it meant that he was nearly ready to explore the deeper meaning of his fantasies and desires. I asked him what he felt the consequences might be if he stopped suppressing them as he had done until recently and allowed them to fully prosper.

He answered that while "it was great to allow myself to go there," saying that he "felt free," he was afraid of where his desire and fantasies would lead. "I'm afraid I might fall in love with a black woman and that that could only lead to sorrow," he said.

We discussed his fears at length, after which I told him I understood them, but that I was certain he would feel less fearful when he fully understood the purpose of his desire.

I had already formed some notions about the relationship of his desires to his past. Perhaps his anger with Lucy for not having rescued him after he had been taken away had been unconsciously eroticized. He could express his anger in his fantasies by imagining himself as a brutal master. But before we explored those deeper connections, I wanted to be certain that he was in the right frame of mind.

To handle his fear, I suggested that he try to stay in the present, especially when he felt afraid—to be observant of his feelings as they occurred, but to do his best to not "future trip," that is, to stop himself from imagining the worst possible outcomes. Our immediate goal was to look at the truth about his desires and discover the underlying conflict from which they originated and the unmet need they serve to satisfy. Staying present to that truth would help him not to worry about the future or the relationships it might bring.

I asked him if he could commit to staying open and honest.

When he said he would do his best, I suggested that he go back to his place at the library and write in his journal about all the ways that sex could be good for him. I told him that I believed his true desires were his allies and I hoped he would have faith in their healing power.

When he returned, he said, "When we first started talking about this, the list would have been a very short list. But I came up with at least ten reasons why sex could be enjoyable."

I said with a conspiratorial smile, "Ten is a short list. When we are done following the steps of intelligent lust, which you now seem ready to start, the list will fill at least a few pages."

He smiled beatifically.

ALYSSA'S THOUGHTS

Compassion

The concept of acting with compassion toward ourselves is one of the most important ideas presented in this book. Along the path to self-discovery, there are sometimes bumps in the road that will require patience and kindness toward ourselves to navigate.

Compassion is much more than an emotion. It's a world view. That is, it's a way of relating to the world that's based on awareness, understanding, acceptance, and action. Living life from a place of compassion not only fosters self-care, but also carefulness in our behavior toward others.

Forming a Support Group

Despite the deeply personal examination involved in following the steps of intelligent lust, sometimes the support of a group can make the process go more smoothly and give it greater focus. I liken the experience to the process I went through learning yoga. Using a book or video at home was extremely helpful, but I sometimes got distracted, busy, or uncertain about whether I was doing the positions correctly. But I benefitted as much by taking a class that provided me with the structure and guidance I needed until the movements gradually became more natural to achieve. Plus it kept me in line by requiring regular accountability. And, when things got difficult, my classmates acted like cheerleaders, holding me to my commitment to advance.

With that analogy in mind, consider getting a group of friends together to read *Your Brain on Sex* and follow the steps with each other. The support, encouragement, and shared experience among group members will make the journey seem less lonely as well as continually challenge us to stay true to ourselves.

CHAPTER 5

Step 2: Identifying Fantasies and True Desires

"The urge to escape from pain is the most powerful instinct of all."

—JOHN LEHER

antasies are a nearly universal experience. A sexual or erotic fantasy can be a long, drawn-out story or a quick flash of imagery that has the effect of arousing us. We may not even be fully conscious that we are being aroused. Fantasies seem to occur at all times of the day and range from the common to the unusual— the point is that they allow us to abandon social restraints and imagine ourselves assuming roles that we don't normally take, such as those involving power, innocence, or danger. Any object or act can be eroticized. Fantasies are regularly triggered by outside stimuli such as an attractive stranger or erotic movie, story, or picture. People generally fantasize when engaging in masturbation or other forms of sex.

No agreement exists among mental health professionals regarding what type of fantasy should be considered "healthy." Freud and other early psychoanalysts believed that sexual fantasies resulted from feelings of deprivation experienced in the absence of sexual satisfaction. Many experts still maintain this point of view and further reason that certain types of fantasies are signs of psychopathology. A fantasy involving a patient's sexual submissiveness, for instance, is seen as a deeper symptom of "masochism" rather than as I came to see it, as a healthy attempt to master unresolved, deep-seated power issues.

Where some schools of psychology tend to treat fantasies as pathological, many Christian groups preach that sexual fantasies are sinful and strictly prohibited by the Bible, particularly those that involve a partner other than a spouse. Both systems of thinking have contributed to our feelings of sexual shame and confusion and have resulted in a cultural epidemic of sexual dysfunctions. Confusion sets in, of course, because how can anyone turn off their fantasies at will? Doesn't understanding their meaning and purpose make more sense?

For many of us, what we actually engage in physically is less compelling than what goes on in our private thoughts and fantasies. We may even use our fantasies during sexual contact to distract us from uninteresting or unpleasant aspects of the act, instead focusing on an image, thought, or story from our imagination that brings us closer to climax. The fact that so many of us fantasize during sex raises questions about the general concept of lovemaking. How much intimacy is really taking place when the best sex we are having is inside our heads? If the disconnection between actual sex and our true desires separates us from our partners, what actually is "making love"?

FANTASIES AND GENDER

Research has shown that fantasies differ along gender lines. In general, because of many social influences, men and women tend to think about sex differently. Women more commonly connect sex with love, while men more frequently detach sex from affection and experience it as recreational. Men's fantasies tend to objectify women and emphasize body parts, while women's tend toward mystery, seduction, and romance—themes that are forced upon us by the media. Studies suggest that male fantasies tend to be shorter and imagistic, where women's fantasies tend to have more narrative as well as greater focus on the relationship between characters in the fantasy. The essence of a male fantasy might be captured in a few seconds-long photographic clips, while a female's fantasy might amount to an entire film. Women's stories tend to have smell and sound effects.

Interestingly, there appears to be little difference in fantasies based on sexual orientation as it relates to gender: that is, heterosexual and homosexual men tend to focus on specific body parts and casual sexual encounters, while straight and lesbian women's fantasies contain more emotion and affection. It's also not uncommon for men and women who identify as heterosexual to sometimes be aroused by fantasies of same-sex partners. Data gathered through self-report show this to be considerably more common with women. Yet such numbers may not portray an accurate picture of the situation, since it has also been shown that men are more likely to fear being labeled as "queer" and consequently to minimize and underreport past or present sexual fantasies involving other men.

Sexual fantasies also vary based on each of our unique personal histories and psychologies, yet our fantasies share certain overarching themes. The most common involve reliving an exciting sexual experience, imagining sex with a current partner, imagining sex with a different partner, or watching others engage in sex.

Common sexual acts in fantasies involve oral sex, sex in a special location, sexual irresistibility, and forced sex.

• • •

This step of intelligent lust helps us to pinpoint the themes of our sexual fantasies and then put them into words and stories. Our sexual fantasies educate us as to the direction of our desires. Yet many of us are not entirely conscious of exactly what our fantasies are. They may seem too abstract or ephemeral to hold on to. We may have to work hard to retrieve them from our subconscious imagination.

Soon you will be asked to answer questions that will help you identify the key elements that make up your fantasies. By asking ourselves these questions and writing down our answers in our journal, the themes and narratives of our fantasies come into focus. Language has a way of making fantasies real. Once we put thoughts and images into words and sentences, we tend to own them more completely. Take the time to think deeply about your answers to these questions. Your erotic images and thoughts may surprise or frighten you, but keep in mind they have their own meaning and morality, which you will soon discover.

After you answer the questions, you'll read about other people's fantasies in order to help understand your own.

INSIDE YOUR FANTASIES

- What do you think about during sex?
- What do you think about when you masturbate?
- Is there a central or main fantasy?
- What mental image or thought actually brings you to climax?

- What is the specific plot or story line in your fantasies?
- Do you think about sex with people other than your partner? Past partners or strangers?
- How would you describe the characters in your fantasy?
- What action are you taking in your fantasy?
- How are other people acting toward you?
- What is your attitude in the fantasy? What is the attitude of the other person(s) involved?
- What sexual thoughts do you have that embarrass you?
- What sexual feelings bring you shame or guilt?
- What are you thinking about when you can't climax?
- What fantasies have you already acted out? What was the result?
- Have you had a sexual experience that you continue to fantasize about? What in particular was so exciting about the experience?
- Do your sexual fantasies include force?
- Do you focus on body parts such as breasts or penises? Which ones?
- Are articles of clothing such as shoes, leather, scarves, or lingerie part of your fantasy? How are they used?
- Are your partners of the same or opposite sex?

COMMON FANTASY THEMES: WHERE DO YOU FIT IN?

Learning about other peoples' fantasies can also bring clarity to our own. The following are eighteen of the most common themes found in people's fantasies identified through a variety of surveys and other sources. Each is illustrated by an example taken from a patient's fantasy or compiled from fantasies on

Internet sex sites. Some were sent to us in response to a request Alyssa and I made on Craigslist asking people to tell us what brings them to orgasm. Use these fantasies to help identify the main themes in your own fantasies.

Some of these fantasies may arouse you. Others you may find disturbing. A knee-jerk reaction such as shame or disgust may actually be a defense against a deeper feeling—an unthinkable attraction that you fear may rise to the surface. If you have a strong reaction to a fantasy, take the time to be honest with yourself. Lift up the rock and search for what might be underneath. No one is watching and no one is judging. This step is about understanding.

Ask yourself: What are the most compelling thoughts and images? Which stories excite and arouse me the most?

Fantasies with Themes of Romantic Sex

These fantasies involve emotional attachment and are like romantic novels in which an exceptionally handsome or beautiful person is overcome by our looks or personality. We fall in love or lust and engage in anything from a simple kiss to our suitor ravishing us in some beautiful or exotic setting. The stories can be simple or elaborate with backgrounds taken from history or science fiction. Always emotionally satisfying and optimistic, they are often the stories that make up romance novels.

Jane, thirty-four: "I have two small children at home so, needless to say, the sex between my husband and me is not terribly exciting. Don't get me wrong. I love my husband. He's a great guy and a wonderful father. But sometimes I fantasize that I go away with a girlfriend on a trip. This is something I could never afford to do any time soon but have always wanted to. Anyway, we go to Italy. One night after an amazing meal she goes back up to our room alone because she has a headache or something. I decide to stay at the restaurant and have another glass of wine. While I am there, I notice this gorgeous younger Italian man. He's watching me. He's dark and sexy, with these penetrating eyes, nothing like my husband! After a minute he walks over to me and asks where I am from. We chat for a minute and he asks if I would like to go for a walk, if I'd like to see the river at night. I know I shouldn't but I say yes. We start walking and it is so sexy. It's a warm night and he keeps brushing his arm against me. He's flirting, and after a bit he tells me how beautiful he thinks I am. He tells me how much he would like to be given the chance to caress me. To kiss me all over. To make love to me. I'm practically swooning. After a few more minutes, we duck into a dark alley and he lifts me up, raising my skirt. We make love and all the while he is whispering things to me in Italian. I don't even know what he's saying, but I feel like it's all very appreciative of me, my body. After we are spent he writes his number on a piece of paper. He hopes that we can see each other until I have to leave. That's when I usually pull myself out of the fantasy. Before I respond. I almost feel like it's fine, normal, to have a fantasy of one night of passion, but more than that and I start to feel guilty. Like I would get carried away with this man and leave my family behind."

Fantasies of Sex with a Younger Partner

Youth, vitality, and seduction are the turn-on in these fantasies. An older "Mrs. Robinson" seduces a youthful stud into participating in sexual encounters. She is experienced, while he is hot, horny, and ready to go. She gently instructs him how to make love to her.

Or maybe it's the younger person who does the seducing. He or she flirts, or acts provocatively, hands touching, legs brushing, until the older person can no longer restrain him- or herself.

Ginny, forty-three: "My neighbor's son is back from college for spring break. Whenever he's home, I have him do clean-up work around the yard to prepare the garden for the summer. He works in his Levi's with his shirt off. He's tanned and sweaty; his muscles glisten in the sun. I ask him if he'd like to take a break for something cold to drink. When he comes into the house, I have a pitcher of beer waiting. I tell him how good he looks and how much being away at school must agree with him. I mention how much he's matured. I touch his arm as we talk. I'm wearing a sexy T-shirt and tight jeans. I notice he's staring at my breasts. I ask him if he's seen the house since I redecorated and he says no, but he would like to. I show him the house room by room until we reach my bedroom. When we get there, he sits on the bed. He hasn't taken his eyes off my body since we started. He's so hot. I sit down next to him and kiss him gently on the lips. Before I know it, he's on top of me, pulling down his jeans. He has a huge erection and I'm very wet. He fucks me all afternoon then puts on his clothes and finishes the yard work."

Fantasies of Verbal Abuse: Humiliation and Dirty Talk

In some fantasies we are aroused by name-calling. Words intended to humiliate, such as "whore," "bitch," "stud," "slut," "pig," which we could never utter in general conversation, are exciting to say aloud or be called during sex. Exchanging dirty talk like "give it to me," "you get me so hard," "I'm so wet," or words like "cock" or "pussy" excite us.

Jack, twenty-six: "I'm down on my knees between her legs licking her pussy. She's leaning back against the chair moaning. She pulls me up by the hair and kisses me then pushes my head down again. 'Eat me,' she says. I do it for a while more, then stand up and take my clothes off. I have a big hard-on. "'You want this cock. I'm going to give it to you. Tell me you want it, baby.'" She starts to beg me for it, but I don't give it to her right away. I tease her with it for a while. Make her suck it. Then finally I penetrate her and come in two seconds."

Fantasies of Forced Sex

These fantasies usually involve passion and force but are rarely violent or painful. Sometimes we resist the aggressor; other times we obey. We are excited by single images or we imagine elaborate stories about being kidnapped or held prisoner in settings like a detention cell, basement, cave, or an Arabian tent. The sex often is wild or "dirty." The bottom line is that our choice about having sex is taken away and we are helpless and powerless in the situation.

Some of us may act as the aggressor in our fantasies and overwhelm a defiant or unwilling partner, forcing them to have sex with us.

Cathy, twenty-eight: "I'm married but my fantasy isn't about my husband. I'm home alone one afternoon. I'm standing naked in front of the mirror, admiring myself, which I don't normally do. I'm gently brushing my hand across my body when I hear a sound coming from the living room, but I don't pay it much attention. I caress my breast, watching myself in the mirror, when suddenly there's a man's hand over my mouth. 'Don't say a word,' he says. 'I'm not going to hurt you.' I can see him in the mirror. He's short and stocky, nothing like my usual type. I'm frightened and excited at the same time. He throws me to the floor, holds my hands over my head with one hand, and unzips his fly with his other. I try to resist, but he's too strong and powerful for me to move. He takes out his penis and, without saying a word, he enters me without a condom. I continue to resist for a while then finally give up. He ejaculates inside me, which I would never let anyone do."

Fantasies about Body Parts

We depersonalize the sexual engagement by eroticizing specific parts of the human anatomy such as breasts, penises, vaginas, feet, or buttocks. Gazing or touching is enough to fulfill our sexual desire. The general attractiveness of our partner is usually irrelevant so long as they possess the body part that is the object of our desire.

Rita, thirty-five: "There's no other way to put this. I love men with big dicks. It isn't even so much the man as it is his dick. I can tell what a man's dick is like by the size of his hands, especially his thumbs. I don't go for men with small hands. I just like how a man's dick looks when it's thick—hard, powerful, veiny. When I'm having sex, all I can think about is the dick. I don't care how he touches me or kisses me. I just want it in my mouth. When I masturbate, I think about the same thing."

Fantasies about Objects and Clothing

Inanimate objects that are not considered sexual in nature such as shoes, eyeglasses, leather, or clothing are the centerpieces in these sexual fantasies. The object has power over us. We are aroused by an article of clothing, footwear, leather, rubber, eyeglasses, or other objects regardless of the attractiveness of the owner or, often, their gender.

James, fifty: "I've always been excited by women's shoes. Stilettos especially turn me on. To be honest, they don't even have to be on anyone's feet so long as they've been worn. I'm not into new ones. In my fantasy, I'm at a party and meet this woman. She's not a knockout, but she's really sexy to me in her red high-heel strapless shoes. I dance with her for a while. Then we have a few drinks. It doesn't take much to convince her to come home with me. By the time we get there, she's pretty drunk. She takes her clothes off, but leaves on her shoes. She passes out and I jack off touching and kissing her shoes."

Fantasies about Sex in Public Spaces: Exhibitionism

In some fantasies we are aroused by the idea of an audience. We enjoy that someone else is taking pleasure in watching us engage in sexual acts. Sometimes it involves the idea of exposing ourselves to attract attention like flashing, mooning, or lifting up a skirt. In these fantasies we might mercilessly tease a partner or be so skilled sexually that we turn them on like never before. We are so sexy, beautiful, or experienced that others cannot resist us. We get off performing.

Mike, twenty-five: "I get really turned on by the idea of people watching me fuck. Like I am so good at it that people want to check out my technique or just watch the way I make a girl go crazy. My fantasy is to win some kind of fucking contest. Like I'm in a stadium or something, with tons of people, judges, and everything. I'm a pretty average-looking guy, so I think that people aren't expecting much of a show. But I have a nice build and I think I'm pretty good in bed. So anyway, I come out and then they bring out this really pretty chick. I'm not sure that I could ever actually get hard with people watching me, especially like that! But in my fantasy it is no problem. So we start going at it on this mat, in front of all of these people. And I can tell that everyone is watching me really intently. Maybe even getting turned on by it. So I'm doing all these things, moving this girl around in all these different positions, and I can tell that she is really into it. I can see the judges nodding in approval. Eventually, after a pretty good amount of time, I finish.

And there is all of this applause, all of these cheers. All of my scores are between 9 and 10. It's awesome."

Fantasies with Multiple Partners

These fantasies take a few forms. We are adored or worshiped by various partners who can't keep their hands off us. We receive physical pleasure that can't be achieved through just one person. All of our erogenous zones are stimulated as we are ravaged by other people who have an uncontrollable desire for us.

Among the most common form of this fantasy for men is to see two women together. For women, it is to enjoy sex with a man and another woman who knows exactly how to please her.

Ellen, forty-six: "I always wanted to try it with two men. I imagine them competing for me. Each one doing something more interesting to get me excited. They never touch each other. All the energy is focused on me. They get in a rhythm, each of them alternating between my mouth, breasts, and vagina with their tongues. I go crazy. Then one guy penetrates me while the other goes down on my clitoris. I don't think that I would really ever want that to happen. I would probably be overwhelmed. But it's fun to imagine."

Fantasies about Sex with a Stranger

Pure recreational pleasure is the theme in these fantasies. We imagine anonymous sex with someone with whom we have little or no history or whom we will probably never see again. We see him on the subway or in a restaurant, or he is faceless and approaches us from behind or wears a mask. We enjoy completely uninhibited sex without requiring intimacy.

Warren, thirty-six: "I have this fantasy about meeting some girl on the computer. We exchange some instant messages and our pics. It's pretty straightforward. I want to fuck and she wants to get fucked. She invites me over. We talk for about two seconds and get right down to business. We don't even know each other's name and I fuck her. We finish and I leave. We're both happy. No emotions, no strings attached."

Fantasies of Watching Others Engage in Sex: Voyeurism

In these fantasies we enjoy watching more than doing. We can be sexual without getting involved ourselves. We imagine scenes in which we look through a neighbor's window, watch lovers in the park, or observe an orgy. Usually we don't play a part in these fantasies. They are like watching a motion picture in which others engage in a romantic or sex scene. They can be simultaneously taboo and exhilarating.

Sarah, sixty-two: "To be truthful, I don't really enjoy having sex with my husband anymore. That part of our relationship is over. But I still like to fantasize. Maybe it's strange for a woman my age, but I'm still very sexually active in my mind. I still masturbate. When I do, I think about other people I know doing things that I never did with my husband. They're always younger people. Once I saw my neighbor making out with her boyfriend in his car. I guess they're in their late twenties. I'm ashamed to say this, but I got really aroused watching them. I could see them in her driveway through my kitchen window. They were really going at it. When I masturbate now, I try to remember all the details of what they did. It works."

Fantasies of Being Worshiped or Worshiping

In some fantasies we get off on being irresistible. We imagine ourselves to be so attractive that our partners would do anything to touch or take us. They are unable to resist our charm, beauty, or intellect and act with reverence toward us.

Some of us are turned on by the "privilege" of being allowed to worship our partner who we view as far more attractive or appealing than ourselves.

William, thirty: "In my fantasy, I'm at work. It's late at night and I've stayed at the office to get some paperwork done. There are a couple of other people working in their cubicles too. As I'm packing up to go, this girl is also getting ready to leave. I always enjoyed watching her from a distance, especially the way she walks and moves. We wind up at the elevator at the same time. She can tell I'm staring at her. She likes it. She smiles and talks to me. I'm really nervous. The elevator comes and we get in. Before we get to the lobby, she presses the stop button and the elevator slams to a halt. 'You want me, don't you,' she says. I'm totally shocked. I don't know what to say. I nod. 'Prove it,' she says. I say something stupid, like 'I think you're beautiful; I've always admired you.' She laughs. I try again. 'It would be the most amazing experience of my life if you would let me kiss you.' She closes her eyes and says, 'Go ahead.' For each move I make, I ask her permission, and she complies until she's sitting on top of me and we're doing it. I get off. I'm feeling pretty lucky."

Fantasies about Domination

Unlike fantasies of forced sex, we *willingly* surrender control to a more aggressive partner. In submitting, we consent to engage in sexual and nonsexual acts involving devotion to a partner, Master or Mistress. There is a sense of freedom, rather than fear, in letting go and allowing someone else to be in total control of the moment. In these scenes, we imagine being "used" by our partner for their pleasure.

For some of us, fantasies in which we perform as the Master or Dominatrix provide the turn-on. We, demand, command, or coerce our partners into giving in to our deepest desires. Sometimes we play on the edge between pain and pleasure. Consensual slavery, sexual slavery, feminizing, and collaring can all be elements of these fantasies.

Jeff, thirty-nine: "I'm a financial advisor. It's important in my work that I come across as confident, in charge. But in my fantasy life, it is totally the opposite. This is pretty embarrassing for me to talk about, but what turns me on the most is the idea of being a sex slave. Totally dominated. Like being forced to crawl around on the floor behind my Mistress. In my fantasy, she bosses me around completely, is rude, sometimes even cruel. A lot of the time it's not even sexual stuff she wants me to do. I lick her boots, even clean her toilet on my hands and knees. She doesn't allow me to look up or make eye contact with her. If I do, she punishes me by getting spankings or by bending down and kissing the floor in front of her, like, fifty times. Sometimes in my fantasy she even has a friend come over and I have to remain like this, naked, with a collar around me, following her around and taking orders from her. In my fantasy I am totally humiliated but for some reason that's why I like it. That's what gets me really excited."

Fantasies about Bondage
Bondage fantasies are a form of domination in which we are rendered physically helpless through restraints such as ropes, handcuffs, or leather straps. Like domination fantasies, these don't necessarily involve sexual acts and are often more about the paradox of mental liberation through being restrained. We are not so much submitting to the Dominant as we are to the

bondage. Sometimes sensory deprivation, mouth gags, chastity belts, or even mummification is part of the turn-on.

Jennifer, thirty-eight: "I have these fantasies regularly where I am, like, sort of a dominatrix. It's totally not who I am normally. I have pretty normal sex, you know, nice guys, missionary position. But when I masturbate, I think about tying someone up. Sometimes it's a man, sometimes a woman. Sometimes I have this whole sex-room thing going. Like a basement where I take people where I have a chair with straps, tables with harnesses and whips, that kind of thing. But usually in my fantasy it's a little simpler. I go on a date with a guy, or out for a drink with a girlfriend, and we end up back at my place. He's tired so I let him lie down for a few minutes on my bed. After a little bit I wake him up by running my hand between his legs. When I can tell that he is turned on, I undress him and tie his wrists and ankles to the side of the bed. Sometimes I blindfold him, but sometimes I want him to look at me while I am doing this. Sometimes I gag his mouth. Sometimes I use feathers or hit him lightly with a leather whip. He is totally powerless. I like to tease him but ultimately I want him to please me. To be aroused but maybe for him to not even be allowed to get off himself. I might lift myself over him, his face buried between my breasts or my legs. I might fuck him until I come and stop before he does or just make him watch me masturbate with my toy. When I am done I untie him and hand him his clothes. I thank him for a nice evening and ask him politely to leave!"

Fantasies about Role-Playing

These fantasies involve dressing up and parading about or performing a role to please or seduce a partner. We often act naive or innocent in these fantasies in which we pretend to be a student, secretary, nurse, tart, or other characters. Women tend to imagine men in such roles as construction workers, military, professor, cop, or fireman.

Some of us play the role of the more experienced partner—the doctor, boss, or judge in which we are seduced by our counterpart. Henry, forty-two: "I'm a college English professor in Brooklyn. I get a lot of sexy ethnic types in my classes. Sorry, I'm not supposed to think about sex with students, but since you're asking for the truth...I have to tell you that I do think about it. There's this one Latina girl who I think is so hot. In my fantasy she comes to my office after class for help with a paper I've assigned. She's wearing a tight wool sweater that shows off her breasts. I can't keep my eyes off them. She tells me she needs to get an A in my class and hints that she'll do anything for it. I would never actually do this with a student, but in my fantasy I say, 'I'm sure you will get an A.' She's really grateful. As a thank-you, she lifts up her sweater and shows me her breasts. One thing leads to another and pretty soon we are fucking on the desk."

Fantasies about Being Spoiled or Paid for Sex

These fantasies involve being given money or gifts for sex because we are so desirable that men or women will do anything to have us. The corollary to this fantasy is that we are so successful that we can pay for sex, spoiling our partner, who will in turn value us for our gifts or because we have the ability to help improve their lives.

Roberta, forty-six: "I'll be honest. I've lived out my fantasy. I married a rich man. I always used sex to get what I wanted. When I met Jim, he was a twenty-six-year-old Wall Street whiz kid. I was twenty-two. I had a great body, and by then I was already good at sex. I knew how to flirt and tease and get guys interested in me. I'd been having sex since I was sixteen. So I'm manipulative, so what? I have what guys want. It also happens that I'm good-looking and smart. I'm the total package. Whenever I had sex with Jim, I asked for something. 'I really need to go to a spa. Oh wouldn't that dress look good on me?' Then after he bought it for me, I would reward him with a night of amazing sex. Eventually he started to take me shopping and watch me try on clothing. It was hot for both of us. I would parade out of the dressing room in this sexy lingerie, showing myself off. Twenty-five years later, he still loves to buy my favors. I think it makes him feel powerful. Me too. It's a win/win situation. I don't have to fantasize. I have what I want."

Fantasies about Feeling Naughty

In some fantasies we are aroused by willfully defying authority and behaving sexually out of character. We might be conventional or well-behaved in general, but in our fantasy we are "bad" boys or girls, acting out the forbidden.

Jessica, fifty: "I am kinda straitlaced, so I'm not sure I'll be able to answer the question. But when I think about it now, I'd have to say my fantasy has to do with being naughty. My father was a preacher, and sex was definitely a sin. He often railed against it. I've been married and divorced twice. Sometimes I think about having sexual intercourse in the pews at church. Don't get me wrong, I believe in God, but I have to admit there are times when I can't get the thought out of my mind. It's usually in a pew at my father's church. I'm having sex in broad daylight. There is this one particular much-younger guy. He's a regular member of the church. He's the one I always think about. I suppose that's the point. It's so naughty and nasty."

Fantasies about Having Sex in Exotic Places

Some of us need foreign locations to feel aroused. Being at home is too familiar or ordinary to get us excited. The exotic gives us freedom to act out things we would never do at home.

Dave, fifty-four: "In my fantasy we're someplace I've never been, far away from Queens. A ski resort maybe. It always changes. None of our four kids are with us. I think that's the key. They're young and I don't feel comfortable at home with all the interruptions. One of them is always knocking on our door. Anyway, we're on vacation and we are alone in a hotel after a day of skiing and my wife is napping on the bed. She looks amazing in her tight ski pants. A little overweight, but I like it. Even though I'm really tired from a day on the slopes, I want to give it to her. I feel like this is our chance, no kids, no responsibilities, and I don't have to talk to her. Why not fuck? I don't bother to wake her up or take our clothes off. I just want to fuck. Beautiful sky out the window, no responsibility. No talking. Just pure screwing."

Fantasies about Intelligence

Intelligence or the lack of it can be the turn-on. We imagine steamy sex with someone who might be totally dumb or dull—the dumb blonde, dumb hunk, geek, or nerd—who we would never consider for a serious relationship. Or we might fantasize having hot sex with a really smart girl or guy whom we admire for their intelligence but whom we might find otherwise unattractive.

Margo, twenty-one: "He's so cute. This IT guy from work. I can't stop thinking about him. He's a total nerd. Glasses, bad complexion, skinny, but he's the one everybody else asks to solve their computer problems. I don't know why, but I think he's really sexy. All the guys I go out with are jocks, but I fantasize about Mark. I never

go out with guys who are smart. It's just not my thing. So why do
I keep thinking about Mark? I want him to make love to me, but I
also want to have intelligent conversations with him. His brain is
a total turn-on."

• • •

As much as we may identify ourselves in others' fantasies, it's also
important to keep in mind that for some of us, our fantasies will
fall outside of the most common ones described here. Just as no
two people's life experiences can be exactly the same, neither can
our fantasies. The mind is an extraordinarily creative instrument,
and the kinds of images, narratives, and metaphors we use to describe our desires are very much part of our own unique histories.

USING THE INTERNET TO IDENTIFY FANTASIES

Nothing has made the exploration of sexual fantasies more acces-
sible than the Internet. With the extensive electronic exchange of
pornography, interactive role-playing, fantasy-constructed chat
rooms, and other forms of eroticized communication, we can use
it to freely explore our deepest desires. Because we generally treat
our fantasies as private or secret, the Internet serves as a nonthreat-
ening way to explore them with little personal exposure. We can be
as open as we choose while still remaining anonymous.

Use the Internet as a tool for exploring your sexuality by lo-
cating yourself within other people's stories, images, or language.
Anything we can imagine, and certainly things we haven't yet
imagined, can probably be found on the Internet. With so many
free sites that offer categories to browse, we can find videos,
stories, photographs of all gender, race, and body types engaging

in sexual activities ranging from the romantic to the extreme. Use trial and error to determine what turns you on and what exactly might lead you to climax, the ultimate test of our true desires.

The overwhelming use of the Internet for this purpose is testimony to people's a healthy desire as human beings to engage in sexual fantasy, while the abuse of these sites is further evidence of how the shame associated with our desires can lead to compulsive and abusive ways of expressing them. When fantasies, masturbation, or sex provide a regular release from emotional or physical stress, they can unwittingly serve as self-soothing substitutes for more productive methods of dealing with the sources of frustration or conflict. Chapter 12 will help you deal with such concerns.

But more than just identifying our fantasies, by following the next steps of intelligent lust, we will learn to understand their meaning and purpose and use them as tools for bridging the disconnection between our deeper nature and who we are in our daily lives.

ALYSSA'S THOUGHTS

Virtually Yours

We have yet to fully realize the impact that the widespread availability of and access to pornography will have on our society's sexual development. If used properly to facilitate learning that can then be transferred into practice, there are certainly social gains to be made, including greater openness toward and acceptance of all forms of human sexuality.

However, my immediate concern is that many of us who view Internet pornography may already feel isolated in our relationships or in other aspects of life and turn to the Internet for some form of connection. But relating to video images or engaging in "virtual" Internet relationships is not a substitute for a person-to-person connection. Virtual relationships provide a pseudo-solution to our feelings of loneliness. In fact, becoming accustomed to forms of sexual stimulation in which we do not touch, taste, or smell may later challenge our ability to find pleasure and satisfaction with another person. Virtual relationships lack the complexity of actual sexual interaction such as the very real presence of human emotion. And while we may find momentary satisfaction as we do with masturbation, excessive involvement in Internet sex does nothing to help repair what originally drove us to use the Internet—our sense of alienation from ourselves and loved ones. The virtual world we create tends be an ideal world in which we don't get hurt, feel fear, or suffer consequences. It fosters an artificial state of mind equivalent to getting "high," in which we feel a false sense of well-being. Only by re-engaging with relationships in the "real" world—whatever amount of struggle that entails—can we reverse the effects of self-imposed isolation.

That said, using the Internet as a tool to self-discovery can be extraordinarily helpful if managed properly. As already stated in this chapter, used as a resource, the Internet can be a shortcut in helping us identify our true desire. My warning is not to get stuck here—to be certain that you follow all the steps of intelligent lust. Doing so will take you away from feelings of separation into authentic connections with other people that satisfy and heal.

CHAPTER 6

Step 3: The Meaning and Purpose of Desire

What Our Fantasies Say about Our Past

"Deep in our bodies is our past."

—DANI SHAPIRO

Where do our fantasies and erotic images come from, and what do they tell us about the deeper nature of who we are?

We have been led to believe that our sexual fantasies are random imaginings, but nothing could be further from the truth. At their base lie fragments of our history, conflict, and strife that reach far back into the forgotten past.

Childhood conflicts produce strong emotions that never completely disappear. Their impact echoes long into adulthood, and even though we may deny or bury them, we continue to succumb to their demands. We act helpless, detached, controlling, or lost. We interpret new situations based on these feelings, unconsciously reenacting old dramas in our everyday interactions with lovers and friends. We lose perspective, blurring the past and the present. We act inappropriately, or overreact; we feel constantly angry with our spouses, hurt by our friends, or abused or victimized by our bosses, sometimes even incorporating these emotions as aspects of our personality. Who hasn't had the experience of knowing someone who is always controlling and angry, or acts like a doormat, or expresses frustration with everything he does?

By the time we reach young adulthood, we have already woven these emotions into our sexuality, encoding them in the erotic images and narratives of our fantasies in an unconscious attempt to gain mastery over them. Yet few of us are aware of the importance of these emotions in defining the direction of our sexuality, and we are even less conscious of the conflicts that originally gave rise to them.

To appreciate the meaning of the images and narratives of our sexual fantasies, we need to review the past to understand the family dynamics that have shaped those fantasies. The emotions that we eroticize have archetypal roots in family experiences that share similar realities. This step of intelligent lust helps us untangle these emotions and their ties to childhood conflicts. We make note of the original outbreak of our wounding and its consequences—feelings of shame, guilt, loss, or fear—for which our fantasies serve as antidotes.

FAMILY EMOTIONS AND THEIR RELATIONSHIP TO SEX

Here is a list of the most common emotions we experience and descriptions of the family dynamics that gave life to them. First, use these descriptions to identify the feelings that most describe and define your childhood experience. Then ask yourself how you might have sexualized these feelings in the fantasies you already identified in the previous step. Later, you will have the opportunity to answer more questions that will also help you clarify these feelings. I've provided a chart you can also use to locate the connection between childhood feelings and the erotic themes of your fantasies.

Feelings of Powerlessness or Helplessness

Feelings of helplessness are a natural part of our childhood experience since our well-being depends upon how our parents nourish and nurture us from the innocence of childhood to the maturity of young adulthood. By the time we reach adolescence and begin to assert our autonomy by making our own decisions about how to care for ourselves, we have learned to trust our parents' guidance and understand that it grows out of their genuine love and concern for us. We internalize that love and encapsulate it in feelings of self-worth. We experience the world as a safe and manageable place.

But when a parent misuses his or her authority in an effort to influence or control our choices, we grow into adulthood lacking in confidence. When a parental relationship has been defined more by domination than understanding, compassion, and trust, we feel less than cherished and fearful of life's challenges. Some of us sexualize these feelings of powerlessness, helplessness, or worthlessness in an unconscious attempt to minimize their pain. We learn to find sexual pleasure in fantasies or acts of submission, punishment, discipline, or humiliation. In our fantasies, we imagine surrendering all control. Where in the past we were helpless victims of our childhood experiences, now we invite these feelings of powerlessness and convert them to pleasure, paradoxically gaining control over them.

Some of us respond oppositely to similar family dynamics. Instead of eroticizing submission, we identify with our aggressor and find satisfaction and mastery by dominating someone else. We're aroused by being in total control, turning our feelings of helplessness into ones of power, excitement, or thrill. In our fantasies, we get off by demanding, commanding, or abusing our partner into submission. We might even go as far as imagining enslaving a partner—a symbolic means of counteracting feelings of having been enslaved as a child.

From the time he was a small child, Mark was given regular "time-outs" for the slightest infractions of "disrespect." Although never physically abused, Mark's parents were strict disciplinarians and frequently used punishment as a means of controlling what they perceived as defiant behavior. The length of his "time-out" sessions increased as the years went on, until, as a teenager, Mark was restrained in his room by a bolted door. Although he protested his parents' injustices, it only made things worse. "Eventually, I just surrendered," he told me.

But paradoxically, by the time Mark had reached his senior year, he developed an unusual fascination with forms of restraint. He started by tying up friends as a game, gradually becoming an expert at tying all forms of knots. To this play he soon added handcuffs, blindfolds, and eventually gags. Most of his high school buddies were game for trying it once. For them it was the equivalent of a college hazing, and Mark barely needed to convince them to play. But for Mark it was thrilling. And, as it turned out, sexually thrilling.

As he matured, he found many willing women as partners with whom he could sexualize the experience. "I didn't make the psychological connection between my family history of punishment and my sexuality until now. It was a way of dealing with the pain of all of that…When I tie a woman up, I can be in charge. It's pleasurable and powerful. The opposite of what I felt as a kid."

Feelings of Guilt or Shame

For some of us, parents, teachers, or church officials overused guilt and shame to teach us lessons, influence us, or, in extreme cases, control us.

To deal with these feelings, we sexualize them, encoding them in the themes in our fantasies. We become aroused thinking of ourselves as naughty boys or girls engaging in secret or forbidden sexual acts. Or maybe we feel excited by getting away with things or its opposite, receiving fitting punishment or discipline as retribution for our misbehavior. We might even imagine being tied up and forced to engage in sex. If we are given no choice except to surrender to an overpowering aggressor, we can engage in sex without feeling guilty.

On the other hand, some of us respond to underlying feelings of guilt and shame by sexualizing the idea of overpowering a partner. We might even exaggerate these feelings in themes of incest or other extreme forms of sexual behavior, attaching pleasure to what are considered unthinkable acts.

In Laura's family, any sexual conversation or even references to sex was frowned upon or even worse. Her mother, Edna, raised Laura and her sister as a single parent after her husband left her for another woman when Laura was just a toddler. Over the years, Edna grew increasingly protective of her daughters. Fearing that they would make the same mistakes as she had with men, Edna constantly reminded them that all men are "no good." She even told them repeatedly that their grandfather—her father—had cheated on their grandmother.

When the girls reached dating age, Edna forbade them to attend school dances and other socials and instead demanded they devote extra time to their studies, watching over them like a warden. By doing well in school, she insisted, "you'll never have to depend on a man." Laura followed her mother's advice and excelled at school. She was socially shy and awkward, and when it came to boys, she was more than cautious as her mother hoped.

Yet by high school, when she began to have sexual feelings, she developed a highly active fantasy life. The narratives of her fantasies were always the same. Just as her mother warned her, "boys took advantage of me sexually." But the idea really excited her. "I would imagine one boy in particular. He was known as a stud. He would force sex on me. I'd resist, but he would eventually overpower me and fuck me." This theme became the crucible of future fantasies and behavior.

During her college years, Laura started to drink, at first socially with friends, then visiting bars and clubs where she frequently got drunk. Soon she started having random sex. "I had to be drunk. The only way I could have sex was if it wasn't my choice. I had to be unconscious or forced. I now understand that getting drunk was the perfect way to have sex and at the same time remain faithful to my mother's belief that all men were bad. I eroticized the conflict. Sex became my guilty pleasure."

Feelings of Detachment or Emptiness

When we suffer trauma as children and don't have the opportunity to process it through the guidance of a loving parent or mentor—whether it's the result of a parent's sudden death, daily drama of slammed doors and raised voices, physical abuse, mistreatment, or even extreme over-involvement in our background—we may become emotionally detached or even numb to our feelings and to the feelings of those around us as a means of surviving the pain of the experience.

We feel empty, blank, dead, bored, or numb, as if there is nothing inside us. We learn so thoroughly to cut-off our emotions that we believe we don't have them at all.

In contrast to internalizing the soothing memory of a loving parent, we experience feelings of emptiness, which is actually a form of repressed grief. When we feel hollow inside, we avoid intimacy with everyone.

Later, when we become sexual, we eroticize that detachment, treating our partners as objects absent of human emotions. We act cold, harsh, or emotionally distant. In our fantasies, we objectify our partners, sometimes dehumanizing the sexual experience entirely, callously using them for our satisfaction without any regard to their needs. We might even fetishize parts of their bodies like breasts, penises, and feet, or even possessions associated with them such as shoes, eyeglasses, or clothing. Effectively, we convert our experience of emotional detachment or emptiness into one of excitement and thrill while still maintaining no real emotional investment in our partners. We create a sense of pleasure, excitement, and intensity where emptiness existed.

When Michael's brother Bobby took his own life at fifteen after years of struggling with emotional problems, each parent fell into a depression from which they never truly recovered. "They felt they hadn't done enough to save Bobby, for which they never forgave themselves," Michael told me. Despite their well-intentioned attempts to involve themselves in Michael's life, they grew increasingly sad and remote. They had little to give.

Michael, two years younger, had treated Bobby's troubles with the typical impatience of adolescence, and after Bobby's death, Michael felt enormously guilty for not having expressed more compassion toward him. Involved with their own sorrow, his parents were emotionally incapable of comforting him. "Losing my brother at such a young age was hard enough, but I lost my parents, too. Nothing was ever the same after Bobby killed himself." Gradually, Michael withdrew from family and friends into the safety of his own thoughts and fantasies, secretly vowing never to get close to anyone again. The loss would be too great.

He kept his vow. As he grew into late adolescence and began to masturbate, even his sexual fantasies involved this detachment. Romance, tenderness, or intimacy never entered his thoughts. Instead his fantasies were, cool and deliberate, with a single theme—"random strangers would perform oral sex on me. When I came, it was over. I couldn't care less about their needs."

As a young adult, he remained as emotionally distant in his life as he was in his fantasies. Although his behavior was not conscious, by eroticizing his feelings of detachment, he brought a little bit of pleasure to his longtime sorrow.

Feelings of Rejection or Abandonment

When crisis or trauma—illness, substance abuse, job relocation, divorce—takes a parent away from us emotionally or physically for some period of time, feelings of confusion, loss, anxiety, and ultimately rejection and abandonment will follow. Even if the crisis repairs itself, we may live in continual fear of losing a loved one again or reexperiencing the emotional poverty of the original loss.

Maybe we didn't suffer loss. Instead our parents were physically

present, but our childhood emotional needs were ignored or neglected. Our parents lacked warmth or empathy, and as a result we
didn't feel cared for, listened to, or understood by no fault of our
own. A parent may have been so self-involved that the focus of
family life centered on that parent's needs far more than our own.
A narcissistic parent can act charming: interesting, fun, or even
indulgent—or the opposite: demanding, critical, cruel, or judg-
mental. Either way, the child gets the message that his or her needs
are less valuable than the parent's. Whether a parent is always too
tired and doesn't have the energy or emotional resources to play
with or attend to the child or she is too busy with work and other
responsibilities, the effect is the same.

In families where a parent has acted overly critical or judgmen-
tal, it's no surprise that later in life, we find ourselves chasing men
or women who reject us or wind up in a dead-end relationship
where a partner consistently places his or her needs first. It isn't
that we necessarily fantasize about getting rejected, but there is
something secretly arousing in the pursuit of an unavailable partner.

For those of us who do eroticize rejection, the feeling can be
expressed by themes involving humiliation, name-calling, or
submission in which we bring pleasure to what at an earlier time
brought pain.

Yet, some of us rebel against childhood experiences of rejection
and as a counterreaction generate sexual fantasies in which we are
highly desirable. These themes often involve romantic interludes in
which we are pursued by extraordinary men or women, or sometimes threesomes and group sex in which we are at the center of
everyone's desire. We are adored or even worshiped for our beauty,
charm, intelligence, or sexiness. We might imagine performing as the
star of an X-rated film or strip show, or as hookers, or studs so highly

desirable that no one could ever reject or abandon us. Through such fantasies we symbolically restore our sense of self-worth.

Rachel, who by her own account had been "less than average-looking," had enough plastic surgery by the time she was twenty-five to turn herself into a "bombshell." Her mother had been a professional dancer as a young woman, performing five seasons as a Rockette. Unfortunately, Rachel had none of her mother's talent as a dancer, nor her exceptional good looks, of which her mother regularly reminded her. She was cruelly competitive with Rachel as she had been with her own sisters. Regardless of how well Rachel succeeded at school, she could never measure up to her mother's glamorous accomplishments. Rachel's father adored her mother and showered her with attention.

He had "won" her over her many suitors, which Rachel believed was because of her father's family wealth. "There was no question," Rachel said. "I was second fiddle in that house. Who could ever stand a chance against my mother? She was the most self-centered woman you could ever imagine."

As a teenager, Rachel longed to be admired as her mother was, but this was just not in the cards. "I was ordinary. Even my friends compared me to my mother, which infuriated me."

As an adolescent, she began to have fantasies in which she possessed extraordinary powers that made men desire her. She masturbated with thoughts of men touching, caressing, and swooning over her. She was mysterious and seductive—a true mythical siren. Though the men in her fantasies could endlessly admire her, they could never possess her sexually. She was too far out of their reach. To the degree that she felt rejected in her life, or even envious of her mother, Rachel eroticized narratives that counteracted that pain.

But Rachel didn't stop there. Through various surgeries, she re-created herself in reality as the character she imagined in her fantasies. At twenty-five, the age her mother had joined the Rockettes, Rachel became a "bombshell" who drew more attention from men than her mother could have ever imagined. And as in her fantasies, she remained an untouchable beauty, never actually engaging in sex.

Feelings of Anger and Aggression

Maybe we hurt others in our childhood. Perhaps we were ruffians or tomboys, aggressive or bullying in our behavior toward other kids. Maybe we were teased or bullied in school or by our siblings, or perhaps our parents supervised, monitored, or controlled our behavior, sometimes using excessive physical discipline to punish us. Whatever the reasons, we grew up feeling angry or "sensitive." In response we acted out, sometimes violently overreacting to situations. Or instead we physically and emotionally withdrew behind a closed bedroom door in fear of the consequences of our own aggressive wishes. In order to survive the threat of real or imagined punishment, we learned to distrust who we are, censuring our thoughts, feelings, and behavior according to a prescribed moral code of good or bad, sinful or righteous, normal or sick.

But because repression never fully works, our forbidden thoughts and feelings make their way into our sexual fantasies and desires. We imagine being kidnapped and taken to a foreign land, tied up or hypnotized and forced to perform sexual acts for which we could not be held responsible. Or we feel aroused by fantasies of receiving punishment or retribution for our anger and aggression. We imagine being humiliated, disciplined, blindfolded, bound and gagged, shocked, hooded, electrocuted, and more.

If instead of withdrawing, we sexualized our anger, as adults we find ourselves aroused by fantasies of mean, defiant, or sadistic sexual acts. In our imagination, we administer discipline, spanking, paddling, punishment, forced sex, violence, or domination in which we transform our aggression into sexual pleasure. We might fetishize clothing, like leather, rubber, or latex, because it represents a tough outer skin.

Ronald was raised in foster homes, three by the time he was thirteen. Child Protective Service removed him from his biological parents when he was four because his parents, both serious drug addicts, could no longer care for him. He was considered difficult to place because he was subject to severe temper tantrums that seemed to erupt at the slightest provocation. Two foster families had given up on him. The third finally stuck with him, offering the kindness and stability he had gone without. With their patience and support, he gradually learned to manage his anger, channeling it into athletic activities, like wrestling, at which he was gifted. By the time he became sexual, his anger had found its way into his sexual fantasies as well. He developed a fascination for "kink," especially forms of inflicting punishment such as spanking, paddling, and lashing. But when he masturbated, he always prematurely climaxed before he actually administered a punishment.

At nineteen, Ronald said good-bye to his foster parents and left home for the military, where he quickly excelled. He responded well to its demands, rising rapidly in rank. He served two terms in Iraq on the front lines of combat where he was admired for his fearlessness.

Whenever he was on leave, he traded his uniform for leather, which fit like a second skin. As he immersed himself in the leather scene in special bars and sex clubs, his sexual fantasies became more imaginative and nuanced. And while there was no shortage of female partners willing to take his abuse, Ronald always stopped short of administering it. The same pattern occurred that had in his adolescent fantasies. At the moment before violence, he spontaneously climaxed, thus aborting the scene. Once he came, he lost interest and the encounter was over. On the occasions he tried "vanilla sex," he never got an erection or came.

As we untangled the mysteries of his sexuality in therapy, it became apparent that it was not his anger or aggression that he sexualized but more the physical and emotional sensation of being on the verge of expressing it. By prematurely climaxing he unconsciously protected himself from enacting it. Where he had spent much of his childhood learning to control his ferocious temper, by adulthood, it was the effort to control it that he had eroticized. Self-restraint had ironically become his main source of sexual pleasure.

Feelings of Inadequacy

As children our sense of self-worth depends largely on how our parents hold and value us as human beings separate from themselves. Our self-esteem, sense of competence, and ability to cope in the world is shaped by specific family dynamics. Frequent interactions defined by negativity, critical comments, and diminishing comparison to others leave us with deep feelings of inadequacy and unlovability. Whether we accept failure as our fate, confirming this negative vision of ourselves, or rebel against it and become an overachiever, the lack of self-worth influences all our interactions with the world. It can also define our sexuality. Eroticizing feelings of inadequacy leads to fantasies with themes involving submission, humiliation, verbal abuse, or extreme adoration of a partner. We are aroused by being treated as if we are useless, unworthy, or weak. Yet, by inviting our own humiliation, we become in charge of it, and through the sexual pleasure we receive, we weaken the impact of childhood pain.

Some of us, on the other hand, counteract feelings of inadequacy with ideas of grandiosity in which we imagine ourselves as important, powerful, or irresistibly sexy. We invent fantasies in which we are admired, adored, or paid for sex; we re-create ourselves as competent, powerful, and often attainable.

As a gay man, Stephen was comfortable with his sexuality. He had regular sex as part of the dating experience, though when he did, he frequently drifted to particular fantasies that began when he was an adolescent. What really excited Stephen were scenes in which he was humiliated. He fantasized being on his knees in front of a man who "made me beg for his cock." He also imagined the man urinating on him, which Stephen enjoyed both as "humiliation and as a gift." Because he felt ashamed of these desires, he never shared them with partners, nor sought them out in sexual encounters. They remained isolated in his thoughts.

During Stephen's childhood his mother was lonely, often relying on Stephen as a confidant and companion. His father regularly traveled for business, leaving his wife, Stephen, and Stephen's sister at home together for long stretches of time. Rather than missing his father, Stephen was happiest when he was gone because neither of them was at ease with the other. From the time Stephen was a small child, his father was uncomfortable with Stephen's femininity. Over the years he put great effort into reforming him, forcing him to play sports and "act like a boy." And while his mother tried to protect him, his father's opinions prevailed.

Of course, Stephen never felt he measured up to his father's expectations. But rather than surrendering, Stephen grew defiant.

From the moment he reached adolescence and knew that he was gay, he embraced it openly, which made his father angrier.

Despite Stephen's rejection of his father's contempt, the years of "put-downs" had seeped into Stephen's consciousness. Not only had he internalized their message, but he had also eroticized it. "I fantasized being humiliated. But I took things one step further. By being humiliated through sex, at least I could feel good too."

Feelings of Insecurity

For some of us, life as a child was filled with chaos and uncertainty. A parent may have been emotionally unstable, alcoholic, or chronically ill, never affording us the security of knowing what to expect, or the constancy of that parent's love. Life was a drama with bedroom doors banged open and shut, weeping, anger, and remorse. In some cases, with no adult taking charge, we filled the void ourselves, assuming the role of a substitute parent, taking responsibility for our siblings, household chores, or meals while we observed our friends enjoying the safe and carefree existence of a protected childhood.

By adolescence we began to imagine being rescued or saved. As we become sexual adults, then, we fantasize about being taken away by a handsome suitor and given a life less burdensome than the one we are living. We sexualize stability, security, and a gentle, loving spouse or maybe marrying for money so we will never worry again.

But, just as likely, we sexualize the role we so thoroughly assumed as children—the dutiful caretaker. We are aroused by being needed. In our fantasies we please, teach, or service, sometimes dressing up as the responsible teacher, kindly boss, helpful doctor, or nurse who slightly oversteps the professional boundaries.

From the time she could remember, Regine's fantasies were always romantic. They usually took place in the beautiful environs of Paris where she had spent her earliest years. The fantasies were more sensual than steamy, often focusing on the same romantic hero, a Fabio-like character, who followed her in her fantasies from adolescence to adulthood. He was tall, handsome, and strong with perfectly chiseled features and dark hair.

You would never know from Regine's presentation that she was extremely insecure. A fashion designer, she owned a successful clothing boutique on the trendy Lower East Side of Manhattan. The year I met her she had her first runway show of her own line of clothing.

Her insecurities had grown out of a chaotic childhood in which her father's alcoholism dominated the household. He was an angry drunk who went on long binges in which nobody's feelings were spared. He said awful things to Regine and her mother. When her father sobered up, his mood grew remorseful, full of apologies and regret. Her mother, having grown up with alcoholic parents, turned the other cheek. Her older brothers escaped the worst of it. They had gone off to college before their father's alcoholism had progressed. When she reached out to them for help, they didn't believe the severity of her accounts. Instead of rescuing her, as she hoped, they too turned a blind eye.

Her only consolation came in her fantasies, which gradually became sexual. As "lame" as she felt they were, she could always count on them to assuage her anxiety and fear. She masturbated with thoughts of being "swept away" by her handsome hero, who even entered her nighttime dreams. This theme continued long into adulthood despite having successfully rescued herself from the family turmoil and made a success out of her life.

Feelings of Loneliness

Fantasies involving tenderness and emotional connection are more common among women than men since men are not encouraged in our culture to embrace such feelings. But for some men and women, the desire for tenderness or intense emotional connection grows out of a sense of loneliness or isolation. These feelings may be situational, such as after a sudden breakup or losing a spouse to death, or it may be long-term, based on long-ago experiences.

Feelings of loneliness and isolation in childhood can result for a long list of reasons, especially when parents are self-involved or over-involved with each other. Often, sibling relationships counter-balance such feelings if we find companionship and comfort with each other. But when we are an only child or we feel alienated or different from our own siblings for whatever reason or we have been raised by a single parent working two jobs to make ends meet, the sense of aloneness can be overwhelming. And while childhood friendships can substitute for our family's lack of involvement, the desire for connection with our loved ones never entirely disappears. Some of us eroticize this longing. We have fantasies that involve love, affection, romance, and tenderness. We crave the feeling of merging with someone, perhaps being sexually ravaged or ravaging. We imagine finding a soul mate with whom we are inseparable.

Others of us sexualize these feelings of alienation in voyeuristic fantasies in which we are aroused by the role of the observer. We imagine attending peep shows, strip clubs, sex parties, or searching for young lovers at beaches or parks. Perhaps we even peek in our neighbors' windows. In our fantasies, we replicate our family position as the outsider, but instead of feeling pain, we are aroused by watching others share pleasure with little or no awareness of our presence.

Terri's parents separated just after her thirteenth birthday. What followed was a contentious divorce in which her parents accused each other of terrible acts. They fought over money and custody of their three children, using them as pawns in their battle. And while they each thought they were protecting their children, none of the children felt safe, particularly Terri, who had always been "something of a loner." Three years after her parents separated, their divorce was finally settled, but the rage between her parents continued for several more years.

Terri's mother won custody of the children along with a handsome settlement. She hated being alone and quickly threw herself into dating, spending frequent nights out with friends "man hunting," then following up her "catches" with dates.

Terri's sisters were both talented young musicians like their father, a famous composer. And while the three girls had bonded while her parents were in the throes of the divorce, Terri's two sisters suddenly threw themselves into their musical studies, spending long hours in the studio or with teachers and other musicians. Terri was left feeling stranded at home.

At sixteen, Terri began dating, mostly as a distraction from feelings of loneliness. Perhaps as a counterreaction, she became sexually active and eventually developed a reputation as a girl who would "put out." But none of these experiences brought Terri satisfaction, nor filled her loneliness. In time, she distanced herself from her friends, said no to boys, and again found herself at home alone.

After months of watching re-runs of old movies after school and on weekends, Terri discovered dozens of sex sites on the Internet that excited her. She filled hours of time searching these sites, feeling more aroused by them than she ever had with men. It wasn't long before she realized that what turned her on most was watching other people enjoying sex. She liked being the observer; it was safer and less complicated than participating. She indulged her interests furtively. It didn't really matter much what people were doing since it was the act of watching that she had eroticized. She had stumbled upon a way to turn her feelings of alienation and loneliness into a pleasurable experience. It only took a click of a mouse.

Feelings of Weakness, Vulnerability

As children we may have been smaller, less athletic, or not as socially skilled as our peers. Maybe our siblings excelled in school and we were considered less gifted, or we didn't mature as quickly as other kids. Sometimes, a parent competed with us, however subtly, over issues of intelligence, good looks, or athletic ability.

Consequently, we felt small, vulnerable, and weak. When we reached young adulthood, we sexualized those feelings that overshadowed our childhood, and as adults now, in our fantasies we imagine acts of submission in which we surrender to the strength and authority of a larger and more powerful partner, bringing pleasure to our longstanding sense of inferiority. Sometimes we fetishize body parts, admiring the size of a penis, muscles, or breasts. We may want to swallow a partner's semen, as if it were some kind of holy wafer that can magically bring us strength and serenity.

Or, as a counterreaction to feeling inferior, we fantasize that we are powerful, dominant forces. We demand, command, and control. We bring pleasure, pain, or humiliation to a sexual partner in whatever way we choose.

In business, Scott earned a reputation as a brilliant deal maker. A skilled corporate lawyer, he was considered highly intelligent, a shrewd negotiator, and, by some accounts, ruthless. By the time he came to see me, those who cared about him felt he was "out of control." Winning a deal had become more important to him than anything else in his life. To his friends, he had grown arrogant and become "a terrible sore loser."

His ex-wife, Melinda, an accomplished physician, had grown tired of both his single-mindedness and his adversarial attitude toward the world. They divorced after a brief marriage and "luckily" before having children. Since then, Scott was "playing the field," dating different women as often as they were available.

Scott was a small man, not more than five-foot-five, with a wiry frame and sharp features. Always the smallest in his class and not particularly equipped with athletic aptitude, as a boy, he felt like an outsider.

Scott was raised in Southern California by a mother more demanding than nurturing, who constantly berated his father for his career failures. She imagined a better life for herself and Scott and later depended on Scott to provide for her in ways that her husband had disappointed her. She regularly reminded Scott, "Your father is weak. People always take advantage of him. He's a loser." And while Scott adored his father for his kindness and affection, he had to agree with his mother's assessment of him.

Feeling his size and background were a disadvantage, and believing that his father wasn't much of a man, Scott set out to become the man that he wished his father had been. He fought against his feelings of inferiority by approaching his life with purpose and discipline that drove him to the front of the class. Now, no one could ever say that Scott wasn't a man. He had achieved success, had enough money and a list of clients that other lawyers envied.

Of course, he was driven in his behavior with women as much

as he was with work, though he hadn't met with as much success. While some women were attracted to his money and position, most were disappointed with his performance in bed. Scott was especially turned on by big-breasted women, but despite his bluster, he himself didn't have the equipment or prowess to measure up to his promise. In fact, much to the dismay of more than one woman, all Scott really wanted was to spend hours nursing on their breasts.

From the time he first discovered sex, Scott fantasized about large breasts. In fact, he had fetishized them. The bigger the better. He imagined himself nestled between them, his lips and tongue "languishing" on one then the next. He would drift into ecstasy while he masturbated to these images, until he could think of nothing else. He felt small and safe when he came, a feeling that he would never indulge out of bed.

Breasts, with their capacity to nurture, could strengthen and fortify him as well as make him feel safe. The truth was that he secretly felt small, weak, and inadequate and had long ago eroticized these feelings in what was an unconscious attempt to heal from his fear that the "apple doesn't fall far from the tree."

MAPPING FAMILY CONFLICT AND FEELINGS

Use the following questions to further investigate the feelings and family conflicts for which your desires may serve as antidotes.

- When in the past did you experience the feelings you've identified so far?
- What were the circumstances surrounding that experience?
- Who were the participants? What did each person do?
- What were the feelings that the participants expressed?
- Was this a one-time conflict or was it ongoing?

- How do you think the feeling or conflict was played out in those relationships over time?
- Did the conflict get resolved? Did the feelings change?
- How does the feeling or conflict carry over into your current relationships?
- What was the most threatening experience of your childhood?
- What were the feelings you had?
- What did you do to regain a sense of safety?
- When did you not feel accepted by a parent, sibling, or friend?
- When did you not feel listened too?
- When did you feel controlled by your parents?
- Could you discuss your upset or anger with them?
- Were you allowed to disagree with them?
- Did you feel powerless and hopeless?
- Were you regularly spanked or disciplined as a child?
- Did you feel afraid of your parents?
- Did you feel afraid of your own anger?
- Was there a time when you felt the bond between yourself and a parent was ruptured?
- What were the circumstances?
- What did you do to reestablish the connection?
- Were there events that led to dramatic changes in family life?
- What were your reactions to the change?
- How did family members handle your feelings at the time?
- What emotional need do you feel was not satisfied during your childhood?
- What is your most basic emotional need now?
- How is the feeling in your fantasy like the feeling you had during a conflict in your childhood?

Study the chart below to make the connections between the themes of your erotic fantasies and the hidden feelings that inspire them.

CONNECTING SEXUAL FANTASIES AND HIDDEN FEELINGS

Fantasies and Preferences	Underlying Feelings
Dominant/submissive themes (master/slave)	Helplessness, powerlessness, weakness, vulnerability
Fantasies about intelligence	Inadequacy, incompetence
Fantasies of verbal abuse (humiliation, dirty talk)	Insecurity, worthlessness, weakness
Fantasies with themes of love-making or tenderness, romance	Isolation or loneliness
Fantasies about rape or forced sex	Guilt, shame, inadequacy
Fantasies about bondage	Fear of losing control
Fantasies in which we eroticize body parts or objects such as breasts, penises, and feet	Weakness, vulnerability, numbness, emptiness
Fantasies of multiple partners, exhibitionism	Neglect, abandonment, rejection, invisibility
Fetishes like leather, shoes, and other clothing	Fear of hurting others, detachment
Voyeurism	Fear of being judged or rejected, loneliness, isolation

Fantasies involving pain	Emptiness, numbness, detachment
Fantasies of getting paid, performing as a porn star	Worthlessness, abandonment, undesirability
Fantasies about discipline and punishment, naughty sex	Guilt and shame, weakness, worthlessness, anger, aggression
Incest fantasies	Guilt and shame, rejection
Asphyxiation fantasies	Helplessness
Fantasies about being treated like a baby	Inadequacy, helplessness, emptiness
Golden showers	Shame, guilt, powerlessness
Fantasies about random sex	Undesirability, guilt, shame, detachment
Worship fantasies	Inadequacy, undesirability, worthlessness, insecurity, abandonment
Fantasies of sex with a younger partner	Powerlessness, worthlessness, inadequacy, undesirability
Role-playing fantasies with a younger partner	Detachment, insecurity, inadequacy
Fantasies of sex in exotic places	Guilt, shame, detachment

ALYSSA'S THOUGHTS

Insecurity

Different people may internalize and respond to similar experiences in entirely different ways, so there may not be one "right answer" when it comes to the sexualization of our early attachments. The important thing here is that you are thinking about it, questioning and exploring and understanding all the ways that there *are* reasons and that it *is* okay.

I did want to comment further on the issue of insecurity because it is one of the more common feelings expressed by clients entering therapy, particularly among those whose parents divorced, which makes up a large part of my practice. For many of these clients, an early childhood experience with divorce continues to affect their relationship choices well into adulthood. And not surprisingly, sex is an integral part of this.

A woman, for example, in her late twenties came for a consultation after the end of the most recent in a string of unsuccessful relationships. She appeared bright, pretty, and sweet, and I would not have guessed by her presentation that she felt deeply insecure. She recounted with some difficulty that her father left the family when she was a preschooler. He was rarely heard from again.

Another client was still silently grieving over her father, who had passed away early in her life. And still another reported that her father met a younger woman and left when my client was barely a teenager.

In each of these cases, each woman interpreted her father's absence as if it were caused by her or, at the very least, an event she could have prevented. As a result, none of them felt worthy, lovable, or perhaps beautiful or smart enough to have maintained her father's interest. And all seemed to sexualize their feelings of unworthiness, seeking men who they sensed felt even more insecure than themselves and with whom they found their value in acting as caregivers in and out of bed. And in choosing men who deeply needed them, they believed there was less of a risk that they would ever be left.

In a similar case, a young man whose mother abandoned him at a young age, repeatedly formed attractions to women who were emotionally unavailable but with whom he desperately tried to connect. He was drawn to attractive women, sometimes strippers, or drug users, who would take advantage of his helpfulness. Like the women in the cases above, his need to be needed had been eroticized and expressed by trying to prove himself valuable. He was an extraordinary lover and friend as well.

While these clients may have felt they were following their true desires, none of them had any awareness of the underlying conflicts that had driven their choices or of the importance of choosing a "restorative relationships" that could help heal their lives. By guiding them through the steps of intelligent lust, I was able to help them to understand the compulsive nature of their choices and to use those insights to act more consciously and deliberately about what was in their best interests.

CHAPTER 7

Step 4: Cracking the Code of Sexual Chemistry

"Sexual attraction is not at all a purely physical event. The soul is always in search of whatever will complete its desire, and our physical eyes are never separate from the eyes of the soul."

—THOMAS MOORE

Intelligent lust goes beyond just understanding the meaning and purpose of our fantasies and true desires. It means using those insights to create a meaningful and satisfying sexual life that helps heal old conflicts and unmet needs. Knowing how to apply sexual chemistry is a key element in that process. This step helps us identify and interpret the characteristics and attributes in other people that arouse us. This is where we start to include other people in our discoveries.

We've all had the experience of seeing someone on the street or in a social setting and feeling an instant attraction. Our eyes lock, our pulse races, everyone else in the room disappears. Other times, attraction sneaks up on us slowly as we get to know someone. One day we realize that we are very sexually attracted to him. Whether it is his hair, his body, his voice, his smell, or his attitude and behavior that attracts us, we attribute it to the mysteries of chemistry.

But chemistry isn't so mysterious. And in my opinion, it's not what evolutionary scientists say—our instinctive way of knowing a potential mate's reproductive potential and whether they possess the right set of genes.

On the contrary, chemistry begins in our thoughts. The subconscious mind reads signals and symbols—usually the physical traits and mannerisms of another person—and interprets them in relation to our individual fantasies. The body inspires our imagination—our reading of it echoes deeper psychological themes. We create a story grounded in our history. This happens so instantaneously that the details remain out of our awareness. When there is a match between our fantasy and what a physical trait psychologically represents to us, we feel the excitement in our body.

If mastering feelings of powerlessness, for instance, is our unconscious sexual motivation, we may feel strongly attracted to someone whose cocky attitude, muscled body, or tattoos signal strength and power to us. But the same attitude or physical attributes would turn us off if the purpose of our sexual fantasies is to repair feelings of loneliness and isolation. In that case, those traits that suggest a gentle spirit who is in touch with his feminine side, such as a soft voice, a delicate frame, or soulful eyes, would pique our sexual interest. And yet, there are times when, on first meeting someone, our hearts feel like they will burst from excitement, but when we actually get to know the person we discover that his personality is incongruent with his physical appearance and his behavior is inconsistent with what our fantasies inspired, and our attraction quickly evaporates. We have misread or misinterpreted the signals.

What do we experience when we gaze at another human body? Our sexual antennae are organized by the interaction of our senses—visual, auditory, and olfactory—and of our perception of what these signals mean to us psychologically. Does the person have the right color hair or eyes? Are they thin or well-built enough?

Ideas of attractiveness differ among cultures and subgroups, but there are commonly held beliefs that influence our perceptions. As Americans, for instance, blonde hair suggests brightness and a carefree personality, while those with brown hair are considered serious and dependable. Very dark hair is seen as exotic, sensuous, or dangerous, while red hair is associated with passion.

Thick hair on men suggests the power of Samson. Similarly, tall or big men suggest strength and protectiveness, while short women seem more youthful and vigorous. Tightly muscled men with V-shaped torsos project sexuality and good health. A large penis means a man can give superhuman pleasure. And while everyone has his or her own opinions about what smells are attractive, gentle perfumes on women and natural smells on men appear to appeal to many. A man's deep voice represents masculinity, and a man or woman's wide smile gives the impression of well-being and happiness.

A person whom we consider our sexual "type" possesses those qualities we find highly attractive, though we often can't explain why. When the right signals appear, our fantasies will be ignited even though they may occur so instantaneously that we are not fully conscious of them. The ability to decode our attractions based on our sexual fantasies is an essential step in intelligent lust. With practice, we can improve our ability to tune into sexual cues, what they mean, and whether they are compatible with our true sexual desires. Armed with this knowledge, we increase our chances of choosing a partner with whom we are truly sexually compatible, as well as our potential to form a restorative experience that will be far more meaningful and satisfying than any sexual hookup.

Maybe we fetishize breast size as a result of the absence of sufficient nurturing as a child. Or we come from an unstable family and are attracted to men in suits and ties or uniforms because they represent stability to us. Perhaps we're turned on by men with dark hair and tattoos. They represent a wild streak or alternative lifestyle—a kind of subversively cool defiance of convention.

In addition, we might focus on particular mannerisms such as how someone holds himself, his or her walk, accent, or manner of speaking, which we then read as signs of confidence, sharpness, worldliness, shyness, or dullness.

For the most part, we register these attractions, enjoy them for a moment, and then move on. Occasionally, we turn them into a seduction or fling, or maybe we believe that the funny feeling in our stomach is love at first sight. Chemistry rocks our senses at their core. It can guide us toward the most meaningful relationships of our lives, even to love, just as its absence can lead us to a lifetime of marital unhappiness.

It's not always easy to grasp the complexity of our sexual attractions. Much of what happens is invisible. The following exercises will help identify those specific characteristics and traits in others that excite the deeper psychological and spiritual aspects of our sexuality—those that create the feeling of chemistry. Record them privately in your journal along with your other notes.

OBSERVATIONAL EXERCISE

The next time you take a subway or train or when you walk the mall, choose a stranger to focus on whom you find physically attractive. Notice his or her hair, eyes, skin, mouth, body type, height, hands, feet, and posture. If he or she is speaking, listen to the timbre of his or her voice, accent, and style of speech. If you're close enough, breathe in his or her smell.

Keeping in mind that there is a difference between physical attractiveness and sexual attraction, what is it about each of these traits that turns you on or off? Which do you feel neutral about? What drew you to that person initially? How close is this person to your "type"? In what ways? Does this person arouse your sexual fantasies?

Let your imagination go. What would you want to happen if you were to have sex with him/her? What role does he play in your fantasy? What role do you play? What is your sexual motivation?

CRACKING THE CODE

Use the following chart to figure out your sexual code. The code represents the connection between the physical traits that attract you, the feelings they arouse in you, and the themes of your fantasies.

Fantasies, Symbols, and What They Represent

Signifier or Symbol	What It Represents	Types of Fantasies Associated with Signifier
Tight, firm body	Power, strength, self-confidence	Domination/ submission, being protected or taken care of
Tattoos and piercings	Nonconformity, edginess, creativity	Wild or adventurous sex
Large breasts	Femininity, maternal power	Acting aggressively, being nurtured
Gruff appearance	Masculinity	Rough or uninhibited sex, domination/ submission
Warm, open face	Kindness	Tender sex, making love, romance
Conventional dress	Stability	Safe sex, being protected
Suit and tie, uniforms	Confidence	Being treated well, being protected, romance, dreams of stability
Muscular arms	Strength/security	Feeling safe and protected, losing oneself in another's identity

Large body	Solidness, being grounded	Being enveloped, losing oneself in another's identity, nurtured, easing loneliness, eroticizing helplessness, feeling secure
Kind eyes	Warmth, femininity,	Caretaking, romance, weakness, feeling secure
Dark eye color (e.g., brown)	Intensity, exoticism	Wild sex, domination/submission
Light eye color (e.g., blue)	Cool, calm	Feeling secure, stability
Sweaty smell	Ruggedness, masculinity	Adventure, dirty sex, forced sex
Sweet smell	Kindness, tenderness	Romance, lovemaking
Muscular and thick legs	Power, strength, stability	Helplessness, submissiveness, weakness
Delicate hands	Femininity, tenderness	Romance, caretaking
Strong hands	Power, masculinity	Helplessness, submissiveness
Accent	Exotic, wild	Romance, adventure, exhibitionism

If we understand the deeper nature of our attractions, we can intelligently set out to discover a sexually compatible partner with whom we form a relationship that is gratifying and transformative. If, on the other hand, we fail to value their meaning and act purely on lust, we risk making decisions that are misguided, soulless, or barren.

RIGHTING THE WRONG CHEMISTRY: KATHY

My patient Kathy presented such a dilemma.

"I always pick the wrong men," Kathy told me at our first meeting.

"They're usually really good-looking, but not classic good looks," she continued, her voice especially animated.

When I asked her what that meant, she explained, "They always have some kind of an edge—long hair, tattoos, piercings—alternative in some way. Interesting, smart, but definitely not conventional."

Kathy's face was serious and beautiful, her slender body, delicate. Her dark hair hung just below her shoulders, framing bright pale blue eyes with dark thick lashes. She wore vintage clothing styled in a dramatic manner that expressed her originality along with the tiny diamond stud in her nose. Highly intelligent and articulate, she had earned her graduate degree in philosophy and at thirty-three was already on her way to becoming a tenured professor at a city university. Her choice to major in philosophy, I would later discover, was not an accident. She had a deep need to embrace a balanced view of the world.

When I asked her what made these men the "wrong men," she said, "They're usually not very well put together." She formed a half-smile.

"They have jobs that go nowhere, no real career, or they're emotionally or financially unstable. I tend to overlook these things at the start. Initially, I'm really attracted to them. The sexual connection is intense. They adore me and I adore them."

"What happens then?" I asked.

"After a year, it becomes like a grand Italian opera. Demanding ex-wives, no money or career goals, heavy pot smoking, and depression. That kind of thing. You know, the usual chaos," she laughed.

"Does that make the sexual connection even stronger?" If it was instability that excited her, I expected sex would grow wilder.

"Oh no, on the contrary. After the drama starts, I lose complete interest. I withdraw, avoid sex, or if I feel I have to, to be honest, I fake it. The things that I was attracted to at the start, sexually and otherwise, become annoying. I turn off to everything, especially sex." She suddenly became solemn.

"And where does that lead?" I asked.

"I never recover my affection after that. I try, but I get really upset and angry. Then they get resentful and it escalates. Eventually it leads to a breakup."

"How many times has this happened?"

She laughed again. "It's been happening since I first started dating in high school. I'd say more than a handful of times. One thing you can say about me is that I'm consistent."

I wanted to know about how her family history related to her sexuality with men.

Over the next few sessions, I learned that Kathy, an only child, had moved to a suburb outside of New York City after her parents divorced when she was around ten. She lived with her mother, Gail, who essentially raised her, though she would visit her father on the West Coast regularly and speak often with him on the telephone. There were financial difficulties over the years that led to their moving a few times, but despite the stress, the relationship with her mother was an anchor that stabilized her life and was of great comfort. Her mother, a social worker, had a second marriage to a man who had no children and was "jealous" of the close bond Kathy and Gail had forged over the years they lived alone. He also disapproved of Gail's permissive style of parenting. "Fortunately," Kathy said, "the marriage ended after a year." Subsequently Kathy and Gail quietly nested. Gail withdrew from pursuing relationships with men until after Kathy went away to college.

Away from her mother, Kathy grew closer to her father, George, an accomplished artist who was living a rarefied bohemian life far different from the middle-class one Kathy and her mother had settled into. After his marriage to Gail ended, George had a few brief affairs. Eventually he remarried too, divorced again, and had since been involved in a series of intense relationships with much younger women, younger even than Kathy.

"My parents are extremely different people," she told me. "My mom enjoys the simple things in life. She's down to earth, no pretenses, though a bit high-strung. My dad's more of a risk taker. He doesn't play it safe, neither with his work or his relationships. He's an artist, ambitious, exciting, interesting, but not very conventional. My mom's more of a snorkeler, more comfortable staying on the surface. Dad, he's a deep sea-diver."

I asked her how she saw herself in relation to her parents' distinctly different lifestyles.

"I'm split right down the middle. There are times I wish I had a more interesting, exciting life, and then there are times I just want to build a nest and feel safe. The truth is, I've never been able to fully commit to either way of living, nor can I say that I have found my own path. I kind of bounce between both." I could read the sadness in her eyes.

As we explored this over the next few sessions, it became clear that while Kathy felt deeply loved by both her parents, each had exerted subtle though profound pressure on her to follow in their separate footsteps. Her mother encouraged her to make safe choices, while her father encouraged exploration. Kathy loved and appreciated them both, but her loyalty was clearly divided. The differences warred inside her and were reflected in the pattern of her relationships with men. Our conversations confirmed what I had suspected. During the heightened sexuality of her high school years, she had internalized and eroticized loyalty conflict, which had then shaped all of her romantic and sexual interests.

Because Kathy had already thought a great deal about her sexual life and had experimented over the years, our initial discussions about sex flowed easily and, unlike most patients, seemed to cause her little anxiety. She said she regularly masturbated, enjoying her sexual fantasies, many of which she acted out with partners. But when I pressed her to make deeper connections between her relationships with men and family history, as introspective as she was, she had never examined what lay beneath her desires and fantasies—their hidden meaning or the purpose they served.

When we reviewed the details of her romantic relationships over the next few sessions, a pattern became apparent. After a period of time enjoying a quiet, solitary life in which she focused primarily on work—writing papers and attending professional conferences—Kathy gradually grew bored and restless.

"I would feel like I had neglected my social life. I'd start going out with friends more, to clubs and parties. I would always meet guys and would start out casually dating. Then *he* would turn up, the ultimate bad boy. His piercings, tattoos, long hair, or cocky attitude are what first attracted me. If he showed an interest in me, and if, after we got acquainted, I discovered that his attitude and behavior matched my fantasy of him, I would be dazzled—heart pounding, bells and whistles, wild chemistry."

Sex would be thrilling during the courtship and the emotional connection just as intense. Kathy's intelligence, kindness, and compassion were compelling to these men, whose lives were often out of control. They welcomed her advice and support. Boundaries gradually disappeared as their daily lives merged. She allowed herself to dissolve into the relationship.

For a time, life felt "whole and balanced." Following her mother's example, she had successfully provided stability for these troubled men, acting as their anchor. In return they made her life interesting and exciting allowing her to fulfill her father's mandate. Without knowing it, Kathy had found a way to honor both sides of her conflict through her erotic attractions.

That is, until the trouble began and what was "edgy" suddenly slipped over the edge. The artist couldn't pay his bills, the smell of pot clung to the bedroom walls, the biker's criminal friends unexpectedly turned up, and the entrepreneur's intrusive ex-wife wrote harassing emails. In her boyfriends' attempts to solve their problems, their attention and energy became focused on themselves, leaving Kathy feeling abandoned. Everything was turned upside down and changed. At first she would do whatever she could to help them, but when the situation didn't improve or the men became too needy, Kathy grew increasingly angry and finally withdrew her support.

By now, it was clear that from the start of each romantic involvement, Kathy misunderstood the true purpose of her desires and had instead acted on her initial attractions (tattoos, long hair, piercings—representations of the "bad boy"), which put her on the path to unfulfilling and unstable relationships.

I explained. "For most of us, our initial attractions act as useful divining rods, but sadly, yours led you to empty wells. What you didn't recognize in the past is that the deeper purpose of these attractions is to help you mend conflicting loyalties and not simply to add excitement to what you often feel is a far-too-conventional life. Sure, your initial experiences with men who were more like your dad, gave you a sense of completeness, but as you've repeatedly proved, it was kind of a fool's paradise. The excitement inevitably turned to chaos and life quickly became unbalanced again."

I went on. "Frankly, I think you've gone about dating backwards. The key to healing the loyalty conflict is for you to take responsibility yourself for creating adventure rather than depending on men to do it for you. Don't assume that men who look like 'bad boys' are always interesting. I recommend that you do the opposite of what you've done in the past. Only date men who can offer you kindness and support, whom you can trust the way you do your mother and with whom you can potentially form a restorative relationship."

Kathy interrupted me. "I understand what you're saying. But I've never been attracted to those men. There's just no chemistry."

"Watch how things can change," I said. "Now that you understand your sexual motivation, you can follow it. Maybe there won't be bells and whistles at first, but you may discover that with stability and time your partner becomes more sexually and otherwise adventurous, especially if you show him the way. In response, your attraction may grow stronger."

While Kathy was not entirely convinced by my recommendation, she took it seriously, and with the same persistence she used in choosing the "wrong men," she went about dating men with more stable lives even though it felt "foreign" to her.

About a year or so later, Kathy met Steve, a successful doctor a few years older than she. He was thoughtful, smart, supportive, but pretty "straitlaced" in his approach to life. They regularly went to the theater, museums, and concerts and dined at good restaurants, things that Kathy was unable to do with less successful partners. They had many long, philosophical conversations about life. Her experience felt "rich, full, and stimulating," she said. And while she had not been wildly attracted to Steve at the start, as I predicted, he was very attracted to her and eager to follow her sexual lead, which, in turn, excited her.

When Kathy last checked in with me, she and Steve had been dating for nearly a year. The relationship is "deepening," she said. "There's a lot of tenderness between us."

"Are you getting restless?" I asked

"Not at all." she answered. "We have a really good time together. We do lots of fun things."

"And what about sex?"

"Let's put it this way. I never bore him."

ALYSSA'S THOUGHTS

Virtual Chemistry

Earlier, I discussed how useful the Internet can be in helping us identify our true desires. The Internet is also one of the primary ways that people are meeting prospective partners. While many of us still meet in classes, bars, at work, or at social events, more and more of us are making our first contact on dating websites or in chat rooms rather than in person, especially young people in their twenties, some of whom have little to no experience meeting romantic or sexual partners in other ways. The Internet has revolutionized the dating experience, in part by expanding our options. It gives us the opportunity to meet people whom we would never come in contact with in the usual course of our lives.

But assessing chemistry over the Internet is quite another matter.

Digital photographs tell us something about other people, but not nearly as much as a personal meeting. We usually show our most flattering images in photographs—perfectly posed, lit, and sometimes even altered with Photoshop. But pictures don't give us access to many of the important signals, like smell, speech, and mannerisms, all of which go into assessing chemistry,

And while chatting can provide some interesting information, we've all heard stories of people who, in person, turn out to be nothing like how they presented themselves online. In some instances, they've created whole identities that are far more fictional than real.

It's not all that uncommon to feel disappointed when we finally meet the person we've been talking to online because the fantasy we've created in our mind doesn't match the person we've just met over a cup of coffee. Time and time again, we find ourselves let down by the lack of chemistry when meeting someone with whom we felt as if we had a strong connection online. It's the rare occasions when sparks may fly and we feel like we've hit the jackpot.

I don't mean to discourage you from using the Internet to meet new people and make dates. But keep in mind that real chemistry is difficult to determine from the clues we receive online. And chemistry, as it's described in this book, is essential in choosing a partner.

Also keep in mind that as our desires change with experience, so does chemistry. When we satisfy unmet needs or repair childhood conflicts, we may find that who or what attracted us may no longer turn us on in the way it once had. We may even discover that the list of things that excite us has grown in unexpected ways.

Self-discovery is an ongoing process in which each new revelation leads to another.

CHAPTER 8

Step 5: Determining Sexual Compatibility

> *"If your sexual fantasies were truly of interest to others, they would no longer be fantasies."*
>
> —FRAN LEBOWITZ

K nowing our own sexual attractions and their psychological significance is only half of the sexual equation; discerning a potential partner's is the other. Feeling strongly attracted to someone doesn't necessarily mean that what they enjoy in bed will satisfy our deepest needs and desires. Whether we are already in a relationship or beginning one, what we learn from this step about the way we fit with a partner will determine the direction of the relationship. What we do next depends on what we discover about the similarities and differences in our desires.

On the surface, sexual compatibility seems like it should be simple and easy between two people with whom there is chemistry, no less if love is part of the equation. But there are so many differences in how people experience sex; it's a wonder that sexual compatibility ever occurs at all. The physical act of having sex, even when it feels great, is only one of the determinants of sexual compatibility. And yet while the psychological and spiritual components cannot truly be separated from the physical, physical differences between partners can alone prove fatal for an otherwise well-matched couple.

Do your bodies fit? Is the size of your partner's penis too large or too small in relation to the tightness of your partner's vagina? Is your body the right size? Are you too tall or too small, too heavy or thin for your partner's physical comfort? What about personal hygiene? Is your body odor pleasing or too weak or too strong? Does your partner enjoy having sex at the same time of day as you do? Is his peak excitement in the morning or evening? How flexible is her body? Does she prefer being on top or bottom? What about stamina and endurance? Is your partner robust enough? Does he orgasm too fast, or does it take him longer than you can endure?

Regardless of chemistry, there is so much we need to learn about a potential partner, physically, psychologically, and spiritually, that we cannot possibly learn it all at once. Determining sexual compatibility is generally a gradual process that takes place during a period of dating or courtship, though we tend to give it far less attention than other factors such as personality, religion, family, and educational background.

After our initial attraction draws us to someone, we usually engage in a flirtation or acquaintanceship that can last a minute or for hours. During this engagement, we are assessing whether a potential partner measures up to our sexual fantasy of him. We are more or less turned on by more subtle attractions that we discern from the intensity of eye contact, the way a body moves, language and intelligence, pitch of the voice, personality, and so forth.

While we are discovering how the story we've invented compares with the details of the real person, he is also gathering the information that tells him whether we measure up to his fantasy or desire.

How do we find out if we are sexually compatible with a potential partner without first having sex?

The answer, which may seem radical, cannot be found in the typical dating guide. And that is that we can take a proactive approach, gradually engaging a partner in open, honest, and frank conversations about his sexual experiences and desires.

Talking directly about sex with someone we've recently met may feel embarrassing or uncomfortable at first, because it requires breaking social or familial convention, perhaps challenging our current taste and values. But such direct communication is the best way to help clarify the similarities and differences in attitudes and desires. If you are already in a long-term relationship, you can gain greater insight into the truth about the sexual difficulties you are experiencing with a partner. If we are to become truly sexual, we need to be vulnerable and open, even willing to be shocked by the nature of a partner's response.

Typically, because of social training, women find intimate conversation easier, while men tend to be squeamish and avoid such matters, though men or women who have suffered sexual abuse may be reluctant to talk about sex at all. Gay men, on the other hand, seem to find talking about sex much easier. Since, from an early age, they have been forced to navigate issues of sexuality in a hostile world, ideas about sex are in the forefront of their consciousness. In addition, as a method of dealing with internalized homophobia, the "coming out" process encourages the sharing of sexual stories. Over time, most gay men develop an ease, comfort, and forthrightness about sex, which far exceeds their non-gay counterparts. It's not unusual, during a first encounter, for a gay man to ask a potential sexual partner, "What are you into?"

The introduction of such conversation usually arouses strong emotional reactions. Some people may feel ashamed, while others find talking about sex unromantic. Some of us are not great communicators, while others may be naive and find the idea of sexual compatibility too complex to consider. Some think that talking about sex takes its spontaneity away, that sex will lose its dazzle. And still others just want to "get laid." A man who brings up sex early in dating might be considered creepy, if not a predator. Even couples who have been in a long relationship often have an unspoken agreement not to talk about sex.

It's not only the content of what we learn about someone's sexual inclinations that matter. How he or she talks about sex gives us important information. Perhaps he is too shy or skittish or unusually overconfident. Or she blatantly refuses to discuss sex. No matter how strong the chemistry, these can be signs of incompatibility.

Why? Because an essential element of sexual compatibility is the capacity to create a healthy restorative experience. And this requires openness, honesty, trust, and respect. Directly talking about sex not only helps us discern someone's sexual preferences and whether they match our own, but also gives us a strong indication of the level of intimacy we could achieve with someone.

Respect, understanding, affection, and friendship are inseparable when two people enter into conversation fully present. Its radiance branches out. If we've come this far in following the steps of intelligent lust, we've learned that it's not just good sex we're after, but also an experience that takes us to a level far from the mundane into the realm of the ecstatic. And if we are already in a well-established relationship, the intimacy necessary in completing this step—whatever the outcome—is likely to be beyond anything we've ever experienced before.

Introducing conversation about sex requires sensitivity. It's important to choose the right time and circumstances, which should include privacy, an environment with no distractions, the opportunity for eye contact, and enough time for a conversation not to be rushed. It also demands a supportive, nonjudgmental attitude. We need to open our hearts and imaginations and be willing to listen regardless of what comes up. We suspend rules of etiquette and enter as deeply as possible into the passion and imagination of someone else.

My patient Julie Johnston did this well.

HONESTY PAYS: JULIE

From the moment she laid eyes on Will at a neighborhood bar, she felt "instant chemistry." And it seemed he did as well. He was her "type"—short, stocky, dark-haired, and dressed down in jeans and a black T-shirt. She was his type—around his age in her late twenties, thin, blonde-haired, and ebullient with an endless smile.

After making eye contact at the bar and feeling like it was okay, Will came over to where Julie and her friend Kate were perched on their bar stools, their shopping bags clustered around their feet, and made friendly conversation. Kate later commented about the "electricity" between Julie and Will. When Julie and Kate finally got up to leave, Will asked for Julie's phone number, which he entered into his cell phone.

"I'll call you later tonight," he said.

Even before Will called, Julie began fantasizing about him. The conversation at the bar had excited her. Not only did she like how he looked, but she found him sexy and charming. "He seemed like a man's man," Julie told me. When he called to ask her out, they spoke for nearly an hour, sharing information about their jobs, where they were raised, schooling, and what they like to do in the city. After they hung up, Julie felt excited about the ease of their connection and more than looked forward to their first date.

At that time, Julie had been in therapy with me for about six months, discussing relationship issues with men. She had become well acquainted with the initial stages of intelligent lust through which she had developed an understanding of her sexual desires, their history, and their purpose. She had only recently started to date again when she met Will.

On their first date they went to see an independent film in the East Village and stopped for dinner afterward. The conversation flowed smoothly and comfortably. They talked more about their families and friends, their mutual interest in tennis, films, and good food. They flirted a little during dinner, and when they said good night at the steps to the subway, Will gently kissed her on the lips.

Julie felt "high" from the experience; her romantic fantasies ran wild. But by now, she had enough therapy to know that there was a lot to learn about Will before she could commit to seriously dating him. While she didn't want to ruin the magic of the moment, she had come to understand that the randomness of her behavior in previous dating experiences always led her nowhere.

She decided to approach things differently this time. Rather than winding up in bed with Will after a few dates, as she had with other men, she would plan a frank discussion with him to see if they were actually sexually compatible. The chemistry between them was palpable. She had already learned that they shared similar social interests and even certain values about life, but she had no idea about Will's sexual desire or agenda. She wondered if it was too soon to approach the subject. Shouldn't she treat the topic of sex with just as much importance as other subjects? She decided that if she trusted herself, she would intuitively know when the time was right.

That happened on their fourth date.

As a writer, Julie had cultivated exceptional observational skills. She reported her exchanges with Will in detail to me as if they were pages from a novel.

It was a warm summer Sunday. She and Will had decided to take a long walk in Central Park. Wandering through Strawberry Fields, the memorial to John Lennon, they ran into a woman whom Will apparently knew. After the two exchanged casual pleasantries, they parted, and Julie and Will continued on their walk through the park, during which Will was quiet.

Curious, Julie casually asked about how he knew the woman. Will told her the truth. She was an old girlfriend with whom he had a difficult breakup.

Julie could hear the sadness in his voice. With genuine compassion, she asked why the breakup had been so difficult.

He explained that he had really cared about Barbara. "We had difficulties we couldn't seem to get over." He glanced anxiously at Julie.

Julie worried about appearing intrusive, but she wanted to know more about what those difficulties were and hoped that Will was the kind of man who would risk talking so personally.

He was. He told her that after three years of dating, Barbara ended the relationship. She had lost interest in him sexually and couldn't imagine marrying him feeling the way she did, even though everything else seemed right. Will was "stunned." Barbara allowed no discussion and left abruptly.

It was an intimate moment. They walked ahead silently. After a few moments, Julie asked if he ever found out why she had lost interest.

"Not directly," he said. "But I guessed. The truth is I had also lost interest, but I just didn't think it was as important as the other stuff we had going, so I ignored it and hoped for the best."

"Why did you lose interest?" Julie asked gently, softening the edges of her question.

"I'm not sure we should be talking about this. Isn't it in the dating rule book not to talk about past relationships?"

"I don't subscribe to that rule book," Julie said with a smile.

"Okay, but last time I talked about Barbara with a woman I was dating, it didn't go very well."

"Why?"

"She got jealous."

"Ah. That's not what I feel. That's how I am. I prefer real communication." She paused a moment, then continued. "So what happened with you and Barbara?"

"Like I said, we got along really well in every way except sexually. To be honest, she was very aggressive sexually. It was flattering at first, but after a while it turned me off."

Julie smiled inside. His answer was unexpectedly honest. She was not at all sexually aggressive. In fact, she preferred to act passively. She enjoyed the feeling of being shown she was desired.

They had naturally fallen into a conversation about sex. Julie decided to use the opportunity to find out more. Because Will seemed so open, she took a chance.

"What was it about her aggressiveness that turned you off?" she asked with an expression of curiosity.

"She always wanted sex. I could never take the lead. There was never even a chance for me to initiate it. She always beat me to it. Near the end, I didn't even know when I wanted it or when I didn't. I didn't have the chance to think about it. Literally, she was always on top of me."

Julie shook her head understandingly.

"Thanks for being so forthcoming," she said gently, touching his hand. "For your information, I like it when the guy initiates sex. It makes me feel wanted. I'm probably the opposite of Barbara. I might be too passive."

Will looked up at her.

"Thanks for your honesty now," he said. "Frankly, I prefer it that way if we ever go there." They both smiled.

By now they had wandered into the Sheep Meadow. There were groups of people picnicking on blankets.

She worried about appearing aggressive like Barbara, but this wasn't sex they were having, just an honest conversation. "I hope this isn't pushing things too far, but can I ask you another question?"

"You just did," Will answered. They both laughed.

"Come on," he said. "Let's sit on this bench."

When they were settled Will said, still smiling, "Okay. Shoot."

"What was the best sexual experience you've ever had?"

"Wow, you don't mess around." They laughed again.

"Okay. I'm game if you are. But, you'll have to tell me about yours."

"Of course," she said. "It's only fair."

"It's kind of boring. It was in college. I was seeing this girl. I would sneak into her dorm room any time I felt like having sex and we would make love. We did it almost every night of our senior year. Then we graduated and went our separate ways.

Pretty ordinary stuff." He paused. "Ask me more questions?" He smiled warmly.

"Okay. What did you like about it?"

"I liked that it was up to me. It wasn't that I was being selfish or macho. It was that I made her feel wanted and she would always give it up to me. It made me feel powerful."

"Yeah," Julie said.

"That's why it didn't work with Barbara."

Julie nodded her head.

"Your turn," Will said.

"To start, I think we have a lot in common. I like to be pursued. I met this editor who really liked me. We didn't really have much in common other than work, but we had great sex."

"Come on. Tell me more," Will said.

"I used to meet him at a different place every time. I'd always be wearing something new and sexy, nothing like I would wear at work. We would pretend we didn't know each other, and he would try to pick me up. I would resist at first, but he would persist until I gave in. Finally, I'd go back to his place with him and we would make love. Actually once I gave in, it was all pretty tender."

They were both silent for a moment.

"Actually, I find that really hot," Will said.

Julie nodded again. They sat silently for a few minutes looking out onto the meadow.

"It's kind of cool talking about this. I've never really done this before," Will said appreciatively.

"So it hasn't spoiled the romance?" Julia asked.

"Not at all. Actually I feel kind of close to you."

"Yeah, me too."

He reached down and took her hand.

"I'm not finished with my questions yet."

They laughed again.

"You're sweet," Will said. He looked at her with eyes half-closed and kissed her.

• • •

By following the steps of intelligent lust, Julie had already learned she had eroticized her feelings of inadequacy as a child, encoding them into romantic fantasies in which her imagined partner showed his undying desire, thus proving her worth.

Julie's father was a well-known novelist, whom she adored, but who cherished his solitude and never had much time for Julie. When he wasn't meeting a demanding writing schedule, he was out on the road promoting his books. She was a gifted writer as a child and teenager, and while she received much praise, she was always compared to her talented father. She feared she would never measure up to him or the expectations of her mentors. And rather than encouraging Julie, her father competed with her. He made it known there could be only one star in the family, and he was it.

Though Julie never gave up writing, by the time she went to college, she had decided to study journalism rather than the creative writing at which she had excelled as a younger person. She felt deeply loyal to her father, settling for a "more mediocre" career than that of a novelist in order not to compete with him.

Suffering from feelings of inadequacy, she unconsciously eroticized them in her sexual fantasies and romantic desires. But without an understanding of her true desires or their purpose, she unwittingly chose highly successful, competitive men much like her father. Powerful and self-centered, they rarely demonstrated their desire or appreciation of her, leaving Julie feeling much like she did as a child. The more she tried to prove her worthiness, the less desired and adequate she felt.

But now Julie's directness and persistence paid off. Rather than repeating an old pattern of falling into bed with men whom she hoped would show their desire, she purposefully set out to discover what Will's sexual preferences were by choreographing a conversation. While she felt strongly attracted to Will from the start and even stronger after they became acquainted, she wanted to know if they were actually sexually compatible. Were their sexual agenda's complementary?

And to her good fortune, Julie found out, that, at the most basic levels, she and Will were sexually and otherwise well matched. Not only did he enjoy the role of the pursuer and she, the pursued, but he also showed himself to be emotionally available, honest, and forthright, all psychological counterpoints to the competitive and demeaning behavior of her father. These character traits, alongside Julie's warmth, kindness, and authenticity, allowed them to bring out the best in each other. They had the makings of a restorative relationship—the potential for transformative sex, emotional intimacy, and trust.

• • •

An intimate conversation involves sharing our own deepest thoughts and feelings as well as discovering a partner's. Each revelation encourages and inspires another. It also involves careful listening and appreciating our partner's willingness to share. And while it's a meeting of the minds, at the heart of it we are all people reaching out to each other with the hope of finding meaningful and satisfying connections. Some say the excitement of blindly discovering a partner's sexuality is half the pleasure, but it just as often leads to misunderstanding and failure. Talking about our sexual desires doesn't have to get in the way of enjoying them. What we lose in spontaneity, we gain in understanding and purpose. Why would we leave something so important to chance?

SEXUALLY SPEAKING

Use these questions to help frame a conversation with a potential partner. If you are already in a committed relationship, you'll find specific advice following this exercise and in chapter 10. Scan these questions anyway to see how much you know about how your partner would respond.

For those of you who, like Julie, have found someone you're interested in, choose the questions that are most relevant to you and put them in your own words. While some conversations develop naturally after watching a romantic movie or TV show, it's just as likely you'll need to orchestrate one. How a potential partner handles these conversations is as important as his or her answers.

- What's the best sexual experience you've had with a partner?
- What was the worst?
- Are most of your sexual experiences satisfying?
- What do you find missing in your sexual experience with most partners?
- Is there anything you've asked a partner to do during sex that he or she refused to do?
- What's your ideal sexual experience?
- Are there sexual experiences you've fantasized about but never had?
- What do you fear most in a sexual experience?

- Is there a lot of variety in your sexual behavior or do you prefer doing one particular thing?
- Do you believe it's more important to focus on getting yourself or your partner off or on the experience of sex?
- How often do you like having sex? Do you prefer one time of day over another?
- What do you do when you want to have sex and your partner doesn't?
- How important do you think sex is in a relationship?
- How sexually experienced do you think you are?
- How do you communicate what you want sexually? Is it more through actions or words?
- How open are you to new adventures?
- Do you like to take your time or prefer brief sex?
- Have your former partners complained or said anything negative about your sexual behavior?
- Are there places you prefer not to be touched?
- What do you like to do after having sex? Do you prefer to hang out in bed or get on with life?

WHEN YOU'RE BOTH FOLLOWING THE STEPS OF INTELLIGENT LUST

If you are in a committed relationship and both you and your partner are following the steps of intelligent lust, by now each of you have independently gained a pretty solid understanding of your sexual desires and their relationship to the feelings and conflicts that grew out of the relationships in your family of origin. More than likely you have acted out these original conflicts in your current relationships with no real understanding why the same themes keep repeating themselves. Perhaps you felt criticized as a child and now find yourself in a similar situation with your spouse. Or you felt isolated and lonely growing up, yet married a man who was distant and cold in a similar way to your parents. Having gotten to this step of intelligent lust, you now understand how you may have sexualized these feelings in an attempt to ease the pain surrounding them. Your partner has done this too.

By each of you committing to complete the exercises in this book, you've already taken the first big step. Now it's time to disclose what you've learned. Here are some suggestions for moving forward. Follow them with respect and generosity toward yourself and your partner.

- Agree on a time and place with your partner to have a conversation.
- Make a date and keep it.
- Prior to meeting, review your journal so you can remind yourself about some of the details of what you've discovered. Some people like to use their journal as a reference during a conversation or even read from it.
- Since the goal of the conversation is honesty and openness, which is essential to creating a restorative relationship, be prepared to feel many conflicting emotions such as fear, anxiety, relief, and excitement.
- It's natural to feel anxious or fearful, since you're likely to be revealing things that you've kept secret even from yourself. Remember your partner has similar feelings.
- At the time of your date, decide who is going to speak first.
- Remain silent when your partner is speaking. Don't interrupt or ask questions.

- Stay present. Do your best not to think about what you are going to say. Be aware of your own feelings and reactions. Make a mental note of them.
- When your partner is finished, thank him for his honesty and openness.
- Let a few moments of silence pass then take your turn speaking. Do not ask questions now. Regardless of what your reactions are to what your partner has disclosed, tell him what you've learned about yourself. Be as honest as possible. Fight your resistance. Remember this is the only way to achieve integrity and authenticity in your life. It's also the only way to move your relationship forward.
- When you're finished speaking, sit silently, and pay attention to your breathing. It will help calm you.
- Make another date for a few days after this one to allow each of you a chance to gain clarity of feelings and thoughts. Resist the temptation to speak about what you feel until your next date.
- At your second meeting, decide who will speak first. Be silent until your partner has finished. Don't ask questions yet.
- When your partner is finished, wait a few moments then tell your truth.
- When you're finished, open the conversations. Talk freely. Ask and answer questions.

After these conversations you'll have a good understanding of where your partner is with himself sexually and also a context for making sense of where his feelings come from and what they mean. You'll understand the childhood conflicts that underlie them and what he is attempting to heal. This information should naturally deepen your compassion for your partner. Allow your thoughts and these feelings to settle for about a week then meet for a third time to complete the following survey. Answer the questions separately, and when you're finished, use them as a source of conversation. If you have found by the end of these exercises that you're not compatible—that your sexual preferences differ widely—you can read about how to handle these differences in part II, chapter 10.

WHEN YOUR PARTNER ISN'T FOLLOWING THE STEPS

When we are years into a relationship and having sexual difficulties with a partner, more than likely what's happened is our true desires have long been suppressed or denied, and along the way anger has become a substitute for passion. With its waves of fury or its wall of silence, anger carries the same intensity and urgency as sex.

Perhaps you've asked your partner to read *Your Brain on Sex* and he refused. Maybe you feel so estranged from him you decided to follow the steps alone. Or maybe you're afraid to involve him because you fear what you might find out about him—or what he might find out about you.

Simply by breaking the silence—telling our partner that we want to talk about sex—changes the dynamic. Conversations about sex, whatever their outcomes, will push a couple into higher levels of communication.

Just the idea of talking honestly can feel threatening and make us feel vulnerable. At best, a conversation will raise uncomfortable issues; at worst, it can entirely upset the apple cart. We may be afraid to express what we've learned about our own desires out of fear of being judged, rejected, or shamed. But if we can keep an open mind, we can put our own desires in context by explaining what they mean and the childhood conflicts they serve, perhaps reversing the years of the negative effects of our silence or anger. We can gently encourage a partner to speak about their sexuality or perhaps even inspire them to follow the steps of intelligent lust through the example of our revelations and excitement for the truth. In the best of circumstances, we might realize that we are far more sexually compatible with our partner than we ever imagined.

While a conversation might not be easy, the risks are worth it. It may be the only way to begin to save the relationship. Yet opening up takes courage, particularly when a partner is the silent type and not inclined to discuss feelings, or when we've lived a life of benign detachment with a partner in which resentment still separates us from them.

Here are a few suggestions that may help ease your apprehension and make bringing up the conversation easier.

Decide on the Best Way to Start a Conversation

Consider location and timing. For some, taking a walk might be the best approach; for others, using scenes from a movie or TV show can be a jumping-off point to starting a conversation; or still others might raise the idea during an affectionate moment before bed. Making a specific date to have a conversation gives it seriousness that some would find useful, while others would feel threatened. Based on past experiences, trust your intuition about when and where to approach your partner.

Rehearse What You're Going to Say

Anticipate all the possible ways your partner may react and plan your responses. Consider asking him not to talk until you've finished or even until he's had a chance to think about what you've shared.

Be Reassuring

As the first step, reassure your partner how important he is to you and that you want to improve things in your relationship. Let him know that you're raising the issue of sex because you want to feel closer to him.

Don't Spill All Your Thoughts at Once

Make the conversation about the idea of exploring sex together. Be careful about how you word things. Don't reveal what you have discovered about your sexuality all at once. Too much information can be overwhelming. Remember, the point of this conversation is to *encourage* your partner to explore your sexual relationship openly and honestly. Let the conversation evolve slowly, only disclosing what seems appropriate at the time.

Put Yourself in Your Partner's Shoes

It may feel like a surprise attack to your partner if you are bringing sex up entirely out of the blue. He may feel anxious or threatened and express it in the form of anger or judgment. He may be reluctant to talk about it or outright refuse. Stay compassionate and don't be discouraged. It's only the first conversation.

Tell Your Partner about the Steps to Intelligent Lust

Ask him to join you in the process of getting to know yourselves and each other better by following the steps. Even if your partner is unwilling, some of the same goals can still be achieved by following the steps yourself. At the very least encourage him to fill out the following survey and use it as a source of discussion.

If all of the above suggestions fail, consider consulting a professional counselor.

COMPATIBILITY SURVEY

Complete this survey. Ask a potential partner or your current partner, if he is willing, to do the same. Answer the questions separately. Then use it as a source of discussion.

1. Rate your relationship on how well you're matched in each of these categories:

	Weak				Strong
Physical chemistry	1	2	3	4	5
Shared sexual interests	1	2	3	4	5
Complementary sexual interests	1	2	3	4	5
Physically fit (height, weight, size)	1	2	3	4	5
Timing (e.g., morning, evening)	1	2	3	4	5
Frequency	1	2	3	4	5
Sex as a priority	1	2	3	4	5
Longevity	1	2	3	4	5
Use of power	1	2	3	4	5

2. Rate your partner on these characteristics:

	Weak				Strong
Creativity and Imagination	1	2	3	4	5
Insight	1	2	3	4	5
Openness	1	2	3	4	5
Positive attitude	1	2	3	4	5
Capacity to state or ask for what he or she needs	1	2	3	4	5
Playfulness	1	2	3	4	5
Spontaneity	1	2	3	4	5
Willingness to let go	1	2	3	4	5
Respect	1	2	3	4	5
Trustworthiness	1	2	3	4	5
Generosity	1	2	3	4	5

For those who learn that their true desires match those of their life-partner, there will be a new foundation on which to build a more satisfying and meaningful relationship. Communication is much deeper; there are new things to say before and after sex. For those whose desires and preferences differ widely, there can be the opportunity for experimentation and adaptation. Part II, chapter 10, provides advice and suggestions for what to do under these circumstances.

If you've completed this step successfully with a potential or long-term partner, you're ready to go on to the next one.

ALYSSA'S THOUGHTS
Outliers

Historically, certain communities had to become more comfortable with discussing issues around sex and therefore have been better able to identify sexual compatibility. Gay, bisexual, and transgender men and women had to confront a sexuality that was different from what they saw around them early on and communicate it in order to understand it and reach others in their community. Individuals who contracted HIV or STDs needed to gain verbal comfort and fluency in order to protect themselves and others. Members of the kink community learned how to describe their desires in a way that was open and honest and without judgment in order to find others with whom they were compatible and also to establish safety precautions. Swingers and those engaged in polyamorous relationships communicated to establish rules of conduct to prevent hurt or misunderstanding. All of these people were the American pioneers in the realm of the bedroom, a culture with a comparatively Puritanical approach to sex. It is these communities that have helped us all recognize the important role that communication has, not only in reducing risk but also in receiving love, respect, pleasure, and satisfaction.

Staying Calm

On the subject of conversing with a partner, I want to point out a common mistake. Choosing the right moment to talk with a partner about sex is crucial to the conversation's success. I've too often seen people attempt to engage their partners during moments of heightened emotions. Creating an atmosphere of openness and generosity is essential. If your emotions are running high and judgment feels strong, wait until you calm down. Otherwise, the conversation can backfire, leaving both you and your partner reluctant to broach the subject again.

Here's an example from my own life.

A friend of mine found pornography on her husband's computer. Instantly angry and embarrassed, Sally jumped to the conclusion that her husband's interest in sexual images of other women indicated a lack of interest in or desire for her. They had been married for several years and their sexual relationship had already declined. Now she believed she had an explanation.

When her husband returned home from work, Sally sat Jim down for a serious conversation. Unable to restrain her contempt, she accused him of being a "pervert" and chastised him for betraying her by "straying." Ashamed and angry, Jim accused Sally of "snooping" and blamed her "frigidness" as the cause of his sexual frustration and wandering eye. They had never spoken about sex before, and now it seemed too dangerous to ever speak about it again.

Sadly, they missed this as an opportunity to engage in a genuine conversation about sex and what all of this might have meant.

Instead, they withdrew into their separate lives, both harboring resentments for a long time to come.

What could they have done differently?

Sally could have cooled off before addressing her discovery with Jim and tried to open a conversation about what it is that he looks at and what it is that he finds exciting and why. Even if she hadn't, Jim could have held his temper when met with Sally's anger and acted from a place of compassion. Rather than accusing Sally of "frigidness," he could have explained how he felt about sex and asked about her feelings about it as well. They might have even discussed their true fantasies and desires. A more open approach, whoever had initiated it, could have led to a new level of understanding and intimacy rather than the divisiveness to which their anger led.

CHAPTER 9

Step 6: Acting Out Sexual Fantasies

When we act out our fantasies, our entire inner world comes into focus, giving sex its humanity, spirituality, and depth. Where in the past we've compartmentalized the mind, body, and soul as if they were separate and unrelated entities, now we consciously bring them together, making our true sexuality a fully integrated part of our being. Acting out sexuality also demands that we leave ordinary time behind by engaging as deeply as possible with our past, present, and future. When we are fully present, that is, when our actions, thoughts, and fantasies align, the sex that results has the potential to satisfy unmet needs, reconcile childhood conflicts, and create a future that is authentic and fulfilling. We cannot fully appreciate the meaning of our fantasies and desires until we are engaged in them.

Yet most people go through the motions of sex, not being fully aware of the deeper nature of things. And while the idea of planning a sexual scenario in which we act out our desires may seem contrived, all the preparations and all the activities that go into creating the experience infuse it with attention and inspiration.

Giving ourselves plenty of time, preparing a place, adorning it and ourselves, creates a sexual atmosphere more powerful than any we have ever experienced. And if we do our work, the experience can feel effortless, even glorious in the truest sense, because it calls into action reverence for ourselves and our partners.

Going from fantasy to experience presents challenges. Our erotic desires can be unsettling or disturbing. We may find them too graphic and shocking. The further our desires stray from convention, the greater our fear and the more likely we are to distrust their enactment. Some experts even argue that fantasies should never be brought into reality because they can arouse feelings of shame, jealousy, rivalry, or betrayal. But personal growth requires focusing on enlarging our lives through overcoming our fears and inhibitions.

Our fantasies may both attract and revolt us, yet they are laden with meaning and purpose, which, when understood, allow us to transcend our own moral judgments and expand our attitudes and sensibilities. Our true desires are far from malevolent forces. Still, we have to have faith that when we align our actions with our thoughts, we will benefit deeply. Honoring our true sexuality is a fundamental affirmation of life. How can we behave with integrity in other circumstances, if we cannot be truthful with ourselves and our partners?

By following the steps of intelligent lust, we have already established sexually compatibility with a partner as well as gained his respect, acceptance, and friendship. At that moment, sex may happen organical. One day we just might find ourselves falling into the arms of our lover or straddling his knee for a spanking. On the other hand, we might feel more comfortable setting up a specific scene or laying out a scenario detail for detail.

To gain the deepest benefits, we open our minds and our hearts and act out the stories that shape our sexuality. We give ourselves plenty of time, creating an atmosphere more purposeful than any we have ever experienced. Within it, we welcome the ghosts of the past.

Some partners prefer the structure to remain loose, emphasizing a few actions or fragments of stories, while others prefer a more highly structured script. Either way we engage all our senses in full action—moving, talking, imagining, touching—an involvement that is ultimately both thrilling and spiritual.

Here are some helpful guidelines for creating what should be a rich, unreserved, and imaginative scene:

- Share exactly what you want, what you're willing to do, and, equally important, what you're not willing to do.
- Create sexual rules and boundaries for safety.
- Establish a language for sex: words or signals that give your partner permission to go forward or to stop.
- Decide on what sex toys or equipment to use.
- Choose the setting. Does it matter where the action takes place? Consider the time of day or if you want any props involved.
- Establish the degree of roughness, control, or pain.
- Create a script, as loose or detailed as makes you comfortable, of how you want the scene to unfold. If particular dialogue adds to the eroticism of the experience, have your partner rehearse it.
- Take turns. Establish when each partner's scene will get acted out.

Any anxiety or self-consciousness you may feel in anticipation of acting out fantasies should yield to the excitement of expressing your true nature. Within the structure we've created, there is plenty of room for spontaneity. As your inner feelings, attitudes, and behavior interact with a real person on unfamiliar ground, anything can happen.

When we act-out our fantasies with a partner with whom we are truly sexually compatible, we enter into an altered state, a realm in which acting is supremely important, yet nothing could be more real and serious. It is a paradox in which we ecstatically lose our-selves to passion, yet remain sublimely tethered to our deepest psychological truth. All the different levels of our sexuality run together, and sex becomes profoundly meaningful, though it may not be tender or sweet. It is a true elixir—a cathartic experience that reconciles past conflicts and satisfies unmet needs.

PLAYING ROLES: JANE

My patient Jane has a younger sister who was physically handi-capped by muscular dystrophy at a very young age. Jane's parents felt terrible guilt over her sister's condition and vigilantly attended to her, accommodating her every need, far beyond what was necessary.

Not only did Jane herself feel guilty for being the healthy child but she also suffered silently from her parents' inattentiveness to-ward her and wondered what it would be like to be the center of anyone's attention. Furthermore, in high school Jane was taller than most of the boys and less physically developed than the girls, so she ended up with the horrible nickname of Olive Oil.

As she grew, Jane developed sexual fantasies in which she was a beautiful enchantress who could charm and seduce even the most handsome and unavailable man around.

Jane came to me for therapy at thirty because she felt lonely and isolated. She'd suffered a string of failed relationships with men she described as "emotionally unavailable."

"They put their work or families ahead of me," she told me.

Jane soon recognized she had repeatedly reenacted her childhood conflict by choosing men who gave her so little attention. And while she was highly sexual in these relationships, she also abandoned her true sexual desires in favor of pleasing her partners, whose approval she desperately sought.

Over time, she allowed herself to enjoy her fantasies and eventually began dating from a new perspective. Now she looked for men who were a better match, using intelligent lust as her guide. And she learned to replace her plain and neutral self-image with one more flirtatious and seductive.

Within months, Jane met a man named Bill. Bill had also been tall and awkward as an adolescent and he also had sibling issues; as a boy he had been compared to his handsome and brilliant older brother. Despite his physical awkwardness, Bill had natural talent as an athlete and in high school was a varsity basketball player. Still, even as his star was rising, Bill felt uncomfortable around girls and developed a reputation as a geek. In his fantasies, however, Bill imagined being wildly pursued by women. His favorite masturbatory fantasy was having a harem of women chasing after him.

With my coaching, Jane got Bill to talk about his fantasies, and soon they agreed to act them out, setting up regular dates in bars. Together they developed a script for their encounters. Pretending they didn't know each other, Jane would flirt with the tall guy, flatter and charm him with compliments, and eventually invite him home. At first Bill would resist, but inevitably he would surrender to the intense seduction. At home, he would make love to her for hours while she teased and taunted him until they both climaxed, satisfying each other's sexual fantasies.

The experience continued regularly over several months, and as they grew more trusting of each other, their emotional and sexual exploration deepened as well as their intensity and satisfaction.

Acting out her fantasies changed Jane. She felt empowered. Not only did she feel her deepest needs had been validated and affirmed by Bill, but for the first time she felt "real."

Although Jane ended the relationship with Bill several months later when she found an exciting job out-of-state, it was a profoundly helpful experience that served to correct a lifetime of neglect. Their high level of intimacy served as a standard of measure for all future relationships.

Sometimes acting out our fantasies falls short of what we imagined. It's one thing for them to exist in our minds, but another entirely when we make them real. And while we might feel disappointed, usually such feelings improve with time and experience. Do your best to move beyond your disappointment by discussing your experience with your partner and planning the details of a reenactment that might be closer to your expectations.

As we continue to explore the nuances and subtleties of our sexuality by acting-out our desires, we stop measuring our actions against what has been handed down to us and develop our own moral code. We are constantly learning to express aspects of who we are with greater authenticity. The degree of intimacy, respect, and trust achieved with a partner through this process is unimaginable when compared to our past sexual experience.

ALYSSA'S THOUGHTS
Contextualizing Anger

I have one comment here—a caveat. While I fully support kink and other "fringe" sexual choices, there is an increased risk of both

physical and emotional harm to oneself and others when participants are acting from a place of hurt or anger. Sexual encounters
should always be consensual, and clear communication is essential
when the acting out of fantasies includes the subjugation, pain, or
humiliation of another person. By carefully completing the previous steps of intelligent lust, we come to this situation from a place
of self-knowledge and self-worth. This reduces the risks of acting
directly out of anger because the process engages our sense of reason. By understanding the origin of our aggressive behavior, even
though we may continue to sexualize it, it becomes much more
within our control. We can then consciously and deliberately use it
to help heal the underlying conflict.

PART II

LIVING WITH
INTELLIGENT LUST

CHAPTER 10

When You're in a Committed Relationship and You're Not Sexually Compatible

I t's not just good sex that makes a relationship better; it's all that goes into knowing the purpose and meaning of our desires and connecting with a partner who understands and is willing to explore his or hers as well.

Following the steps of intelligent lust together fosters friendship—a special kind of connection based on intimacy, respect, and courage that provides a loving context for handling whatever discoveries emerge.

Sadly, some couples may discover they are not sexually compatible, or one spouse may not be prepared to act out what he or she has discovered or may wish to keep his or her fantasies as private. Even so, having a deeper understanding of the real source of their differences may enable those couples to come to terms with them. This doesn't necessarily mean the relationship is over. On the contrary, after a period of acknowledging and accepting the truth, partners realize that choices can be made. New roads can open to fulfillment. Some agree to continue the marriage without sex because they feel other areas of compatibility issues matter more; others make an attempt to consciously address their partner's sexual needs and actually find joy in the act of giving; some take an unconventional approach and consider open relationships, three-ways, or partner swapping, all of which have the potential to strengthen a partnership. And a few choose to end the marriage, knowing the decision was made for the right reasons.

Three couples I worked with in therapy came to different solutions for handling the challenges that sex presented to their relationships. A fourth couple, the last, was treated by Alyssa.

REDISCOVERING SEXUAL COMPATIBILITY: HANK AND MARION

Hank took Marion to a health spa for a weekend of renewal including healthy food, massage, and meditation. It was part of their decision to trade their ambitious, fast-paced lives as dual-career lawyers and doting parents, for lives that were "better balanced," as Hank put it. Hank also had another agenda. He planned to use the opportunity to raise the issue of sex, which had been troubling him for some time. They had been married eight years and for the last three had only been sexual a dozen or so times. While they were sexually active in their early years of marriage, they had become single-mindedly focused on their jobs, working late hours and social networking. They were also raising two demanding children, which usually left them "too exhausted to even think about sex." At least that's what they told themselves and each other.

The truth was that Hank was more frustrated than he let on to Marion. He was also very close to having an affair when he came to see me for therapy two months earlier. He had been flirting with a colleague for more than six months but had just recently stopped short of spending the night with her.

"I love my wife," he told me. "She doesn't deserve that and neither do I. I'm not sure I could live with myself afterwards. But, frankly, sex with my wife sucks."

"What does Marion say about it?" I asked.

"She doesn't say much. She makes excuses like, 'I'm exhausted; the kids are still awake; I have this brief to finish.' That's all true, but I don't want to give up sex for the next ten years until our kids are grown up." He lowered his eyes.

"What's it like when you do have sex?" I asked.

"She's just not there. She doesn't seem interested. It feels like she just wants to get it over with."

"What was sex like before you had children?" I wanted to track the history to determine whether the problem existed before their lives had grown so busy. My question proved useful.

"To be honest, we had a lot of sex when we first got together. But it went stale after a couple of years. I think the problem was there before the kids came. But we were both pretty single-minded about our careers and ignored it. We let sex drift away. Neither of us complained. Sometimes we would have sex just to remind ourselves that we were still capable of it."

"Why does it matter now?" I asked curiously.

"Well I gained a lot of weight during the marriage. You wouldn't know that by looking at me now. About a year ago, I started going to the gym. I lost all the weight I gained and more. I got in very good shape. Women started to notice me again, and I started feeling sexual."

"Did you try to reintroduce sex with Marion at that time?"

"Yep, but it didn't go anywhere. She got resentful. I initiated sex quite a few times, but essentially, she rejected me and I decided I didn't want to push her into something she didn't want to do. What would be the point of that?"

"Did you talk about your feelings with her then?"

"No, I didn't know how. I'm no prude, but talking about sex just isn't part of my vocabulary."

Though they were both highly educated and successful people, it seemed clear that sex was a touchy subject. Neither seemed capable of engaging in a productive conversation about it, though I didn't understand the specific reasons why yet. I felt the most useful way to help Hank would be to include Marion in following the steps of intelligent lust right from the start. Since they had already determined to lead healthier lives, I suggested that Hank and Marion come to therapy together as part of that project.

"I don't want her to feel ambushed by us into a conversation, so I would like for you to speak to her about sex first," I said.

I coached Hank on how best to bring up the issue using the guidelines presented in this book. Hank agreed, and a few months later, after he and Marion had spent the weekend away, he called to arrange an appointment.

"What did Hank tell you about coming here?" I asked during the first few minutes of our initial session together.

"He told me that he would like us to work on our sexual relationship. He didn't say much else."

"How do you feel about that?"

"I think he's right."

"How do *you* imagine doing that?"

"We'll just set aside time after the kids are asleep and get it done."

Her manner of speaking was efficient; her words seemed re-hearsed. Since I had seen her husband alone, I imagined that some of her anxiety could be attributed to her concern about what I had already been told. The fact was that Hank had admitted he had a "flirtation," and he and I held that secret. I wasn't certain if it was necessary to raise the issue, but I made the decision then that it wouldn't be in either's best interest at that time.

"I'm a morning person," Hank said with a half-smile.

Marion imitated his smile. "I'm not and I certainly don't want to get up any earlier to have sex." She was clearly annoyed.

"You never want to have sex," Hank responded.

They sat silently for a moment, then I spoke up. "Imagine for a moment, that the problem wasn't that you were busy and exhaust-ed, that you were relaxed and comfortable at home. What would the problem with sex be then?" I was addressing both of them.

"Tell him what you told me over the weekend," Hank said shyly.

She sat silently as if she were resisting his request.

Hank filled in the silence. "She told me I was too aggressive. That I just thought of myself—about what I wanted…"

"I said you weren't a particularly sensitive lover," she said, clari-fying the meaning.

"What's your reaction to that?" I asked Hank.

"I was surprised. I thought I was taking care of her."

"On your terms as always," Marion said, raising her voice.

I asked her to explain.

"It's the same as with everything else in our lives. It has to be on his terms. How, when, what we do. It's all his way. It's no different with sex."

"Honestly, I thought that's what you wanted."

"Come on, Hank, how could you not know what I want?"

"We never talked about it. I just assumed…"

"I wonder," I said to Marion, "what would your terms be regarding sex?"

"I'm glad someone asked. That's never happened before."

Hank looked embarrassed. "I just assumed she wanted me to be in charge. We're both strong-willed, but in the bedroom I just figured, I'm the guy, I take over."

"What century are you living in?" Marion quipped.

"Okay, okay. I get it. I just didn't know that's what you wanted." He stood accused and convicted.

I returned to my original question to Marion. "How do you want sex to be?" I asked her gently.

"I don't really know. I've never had the chance to think about it. He's always pushing himself on me."

"Fair enough," I said. "But can you think about it now?"

She thought for a minute, then looked at me directly and said, "I'm not sure where this is going. Therapy is his idea."

I nodded my head in agreement. "Do you have another way?"

She dropped her guard and for a tender moment I could see the hurt child. "No."

"Let's give this a try then," I said.

Her hostility seemed to ease slightly. I made the leap. I explained the first step of intelligent lust and sent them home with the task that each independently thinks about their fantasies and what their true sexual desires might be.

When they returned a week later, Marion said that she had difficulty staying focused on the assignment since she could barely get any private time. Again, she seemed angry.

"When you did have time to think about it, what came into your mind?" I asked gently.

"I don't know that I want to share it with you or Hank for that matter."

"How are we going to get anywhere if you don't participate?" Hank insisted.

"Listen," she said. "Going to therapy is your idea. Again, everything is on your terms." Her guard was back up.

Hank looked at me helplessly.

"Is there a way we can continue to talk that would make you feel more comfortable?" I said, respectfully giving her control of the conversation.

"I'm sorry," she said. "I just don't get the premise of this. I really don't want to talk about my fantasies. The point is that Hank is controlling and I want him to stop."

"And if he stops?" I asked.

"I already have," Hank said, jumping in. "I heard what you said last week. And I got it. I really paid attention to how I am with you. I think you're right." He paused. "Now it's up to you. Tell me what to do."

"Ugh. Another demand," she said.

"Let's not do another round of this," I said pleadingly.

"You're right," she said, softening a bit. "Let's not do this again." She paused long enough to rethink her approach.

"Okay. My fantasy is not that complicated. I want to be made love to. Not overwhelmed, not taken, made love to. Not controlled. Soft, tender, sweet, as if I were a d-e-l-i-c-a-t-e creature." She spelled the word out for emphasis.

Hank looked surprised. He reached over to touch her arm, but she gently pushed his hand away.

"I honestly thought you liked me being aggressive. I don't want to hurt you, but, I mean, you're often combative. You've told me more than once that I was the only one who ever stood up to you."

"Yes, that's true. It's why I married you. But there's a difference in being strong and being controlling and selfish. Especially in bed. You asked me my fantasy and that's what it is."

There was silence.

"I'm relieved," Hank finally said. "I'd love to drop my guard and relax with you even for a minute. Just be together with no pressure. I've always felt like I had to perform—to be strong. I wouldn't mind some tenderness myself. When I did the homework, what I imagined was very sweet and gentle. I was the romantic hero, the prince, shining knight. You know."

By the end of that session, the hostility between them had palpably changed. The sword hand been dropped and they actually were communicating what they felt. I suggested that they not attempt to have sex while we were exploring the issues, but for homework that week I asked them to think about childhood experiences in which they had similar experiences to what they felt in the marriage. I said to Marion, "Think about those times when you needed to protect and defend yourself." Marion laughed.

"When didn't I have to protect myself?" she said.

When I asked what she meant, she said, "I grew up in a really hostile household. Lots of fighting. Believe me, I never rested."

The next, week when they returned, the atmosphere between them was decidedly warmer. Marion said that she did her homework and could remember having a lot of daydreams as a child and teenager about being saved from the hostilities at home by a kindly stranger. When we talked about how she might have eroticized those feelings, she remembered that her earliest sexual fantasies were of being rescued by a handsome stranger, "I know it's a cliché, but a kind of knight-in-shining-armor who took me away." These fantasies continued through her adult years until, overwhelmed with ambition and responsibility, she stopped thinking about sex altogether. For the first time, she revealed the vulnerable child hidden behind her guardedness and the secret fantasy of being rescued from the war zone that was her parental home.

Hank, on the other hand, had grown up with two "kind, but ineffectual parents" who spent long days at underpaid jobs at the same manufacturing company where they had worked for thirty years. "Never the type to complain," though their sacrifice was obvious, they raised four children on a very tight budget, rarely earning enough money to enjoy even the simplest pleasures of life. A devoted son, Hank remembers making a vow as a teenager to find a way to make his parents' lives easier—to eventually rescue them from their economic hardships.

"I became a lawyer mostly for them. I knew I'd make great money and be able to help them." When we talked about these feelings in connection to sex, he remembered that during his childhood he was preoccupied with "superheroes who rescued victims from villains." As he put the pieces of the sexual puzzle together, he recognized that during his teens, he had eroticized those feelings in fantasies in which he also played the hero, sometimes even wearing tights and a cape.

Through our discussions over the next few sessions, Hank began to understand that Marion needed a hero too, and it wasn't the tough guy he assumed it would be. He felt excited, even aroused by the idea that he could be her hero by acting more like a gentle lover.

In our last sessions both were more lighthearted. They seemed to appreciate their discovery—how sexually compatible they actually were. "I always knew we were meant for each other," he said. "I just had the wrong approach."

Finally, I coached them on how to enact their fantasies, including capes, tights, and more.

CREATING AN OPEN RELATIONSHIP: JAMES AND ROBERT

As a same-sex couple, James and Robert were left to negotiate the division of roles in their relationship without any visible role models or maps to follow. Over time, they chose responsibilities that were best suited for them rather than ones decided by gender as often happens in heterosexual relationships. James paid the bills and did most of the cooking. Robert acted as handyman and did more of the household chores.

Together for five years, they celebrated their commitment in a ceremony two years before they came to see me for therapy. Like many gay men, sex had been in their consciousness from the time when they first had a sense of their "differentness." By the time they met when James was thirty-eight and Robert, thirty-four, both had many sexual experiences and a few short relationships through which they refined their sexual tastes and preferences. James enjoyed sex most as a "dominant top," with "straight-acting" though sexually passive men. Robert also liked topping, though he preferred sex with men who were aggressive bottoms who would ultimately surrender to him.

Their courtship was slow. They met playing rugby on opposing teams in a national gay league. They took time getting to know each other, each alternately organizing weekly dates planned around cultural life in New York. They were physically attracted to each other but took sex slowly too. When they finally had sex after a few months of dating, they had already developed serious feelings for each other. Sex was more than recreational.

Robert was more flexible sexually and, at first, willing to bottom for James, though he also preferred being the top. Since everything else in the relationship "seemed great," Robert continued to go along with sex as it was, occasionally complaining about the lack of James's sexual versatility. At those times, James would try to bottom, but "it never really worked" and they would quickly return to old habits. Over time, sex between them became less frequent.

Otherwise, they created a warm, supportive family of friends whom they enjoyed entertaining. Both became excellent cooks and they competed to outshine the other's talent in the kitchen, but always with a sense of humor and goodwill.

Secretly though, Robert had slowly been building resentment. Then one evening, according to James, "he went ballistic about sex," shocking James and himself, particularly because they rarely had a cross word.

"I had a tantrum about how rigid James is sexually," Robert said. Afterward, they had several calmer, though serious, conversations in which they discussed the problem and possible solutions. That's when they requested a consultation with me.

"We're not very sexually compatible," they both agreed. When I asked them how they were so certain, James offered, "It's just not working with sex. We don't enjoy the same things or more accurately, we both enjoy doing the same thing. I know what I'm into and what works for me. I don't enjoy getting fucked and neither does Bobby. We love each other and have a lot in common. We have a great life together, but sex is a big problem."

"We don't want to break up," added Robert, "but neither of us is about to give up having sex for the rest of our lives. So what we decided was to open up the relationship to sex with other men."

"We need your help figuring out the rules," James said.

Since they seemed so certain of their sexual desires, having gone through the equivalent steps of intelligent lust independently, I agreed to help them negotiate a plan for how they could open their relationship to other sexual partners with honesty and respect. I started by asking what they each imagined as their ideal situation.

"Occasionally, I'd like to hook up with men I meet at the gym or online," Robert answered.

"How often is occasionally?" I asked.

"That's hard to say. Maybe every few weeks. I don't know; whenever it happens."

"That sounds like more than occasionally," James said.

"I guess you're right," he laughed. "How about regularly then?"

They both laughed now. "Don't get me wrong. I like sex a lot, but I don't want either of us to be spending all our free time on the Internet fishing for men," James added.

"Neither do I," Robert said sweetly. "I love the time we spend together. This isn't about that."

"What about starting with three-ways?" James asked.

"Nope. I don't think that would work. I don't mind your having sex with other men, but I'm not ready yet to watch you. Maybe down the road, but not now. How about we limit it to once a month unless someone great turns up?"

James nodded.

"Do you want each other to know when you're planning on having sex, or after you've had sex? Do you want to know who it's going to be with, or should it be a 'don't ask, don't tell' policy?" I asked.

"I want to know," said James. "I would rather we are up front and deal with the truth."

"Agreed," said Robert. "Sneaking around won't work. But this is going to take a lot of trust. I would actually like it if we ask each other for permission before we hook up."

"Hmmm. What? Call you and ask if it's okay? That might be a little weird. 'Excuse me, Frank, while I call my boyfriend and see if it's okay to fuck you.'"

They both laughed.

"Here's what I think," James said. "We can change it later if we want, but I don't think we should have to ask for permission so long as it doesn't interfere with being together. No breaking plans to have sex. Giving each other permission feels too parental." He turned to me. "Any suggestions?"

I thought a moment, and then answered. "Yes. Most people who succeed at open relationships care deeply about their primary partner, which seems to be the situation between the two of you. I understand your concern about asking permission each time, but I think since you're doing this out of deep respect for each other's needs, the most challenging part of this will be to preserve those feelings of respect. Some people ask how their partner feels about them having sex with someone else each time. That's not the same as asking permission, but it does give each of you the opportunity to say, 'That's not cool right now,' if there is some reason you can't handle it at that moment. There are a lot of surprises when you open up a relationship, and I think it's best when partners navigate one event at a time."

They both nodded their heads in agreement.

"It's a subtle distinction you're making. Asking about how Robert feels versus asking for his permission," James said. "I get your point."

"I like the idea," Robert added.

"What else do we need to think about?" James asked.

"There's always a risk of becoming involved or attached to a sexual partner," I said. "I suppose that will be the true test of your feelings for each other. Some people make rules to try and to avoid that."

"What kind of rules?" James asked.

"Like never seeing the same person more than once."

"I like that idea," James said.

"I do too."

"What about bringing someone home?" I asked.

"I'm against that. I don't want strangers coming into the house." James agreed.

"And what about overnights?" I asked.

"I definitely don't think we should stay overnight with anyone else either," Robert answered.

"One last thing then," I said. "Where do you stand with safe sex?"

"We always have safe sex with each other—condoms only. I don't think that's an issue," Robert said. "Do you?"

"Of course not. We're both thankfully HIV negative and that's not going to change. We're not self-destructive."

We ended the session with a symbolic gentlemen's handshake, affirming the boundaries set forth.

When we met again three months later, Robert and James talked openly about their experiences. Both had honored the rules, and except for a few instances of rivalry in which Robert felt competitive with James because he was "getting hit on more frequently," things seemed to have gone well. We talked about feelings of jealousy, but neither experienced anything strong enough to have raised it as an issue. In fact, they both agreed there was less resentment and tension in the relationship, and they were better off for having opened it.

"What have you learned about yourselves during these months?" I asked.

"It's more what I learned about Robert," James answered. "He's really enjoying himself. I want that for him. I don't feel threatened in any way. What he does has nothing to do with how he feels about me. In fact, what we're doing really speaks to the strength of our relationship. It doesn't feel fake. I mean, you have to really love someone to work through this stuff. We have nothing holding us together, no marriage license, nothing but how we feel about each other every day."

Robert smiled genuinely.

CROSSING CONVENTIONAL BOUNDARIES TOGETHER: MARGOT AND BILLY

Like most couples, Margot and Billy had married without much discussion of sex. For the two years since, both imagined the other enjoyed their lovemaking, though privately each felt detached and unsatisfied. They cared about each other deeply, got along well in most ways, and shared similar values about life. But without honest communication about sex, which each withheld for fear of upsetting the other, they had grown quietly more distant.

When Margot, with my encouragement, finally asked Billy if they could talk about their sex lives, he actually felt relieved. Since then, they've had regular conversations in which they followed the steps of intelligent lust. Each had come to recognize what he or she had eroticized earlier in their lives as well as the meaning behind those desires.

Margot's mother was a ballet dancer who retired after a knee injury. She had pinned her hopes on her only daughter, pushing her into ballet class and local performances at an early age. She called on Margot, who was by nature shy and reluctant, at every social occasion to dance for friends and family. "Frankly," Margot told me, "I had no talent and no interest, but that never stopped my mother. She was determined for me to be the star she never was."

By the time Margot reached adolescence, she resented both dance and her mother's control. Despite these feelings, she began daydreaming about performing for school friends and boys from the neighborhood. She had read the story of Salome for a school project and imagined herself as the beautiful seductress, dancing with her seven veils. Gradually, her daydreams became sexual fantasies in which she imagined herself dancing naked in front of men. Without knowing it, she had eroticized the painful feelings that surrounded her mother's demands, bringing instead deep pleasure to the very thing she feared and hated. As she grew into adulthood, the majority of her masturbatory fantasies focused on having sex while being watched. Yet, because these fantasies also felt as if she were surrendering to her mother, she made a decision to avoid sex altogether and, therefore, rarely engaged in it.

"No one would know it," Margot said to me early in our therapy. "If I would let myself go, I would be a full-blown exhibitionist."

Billy, on the other hand, felt invisible as a child. He was the middle of five siblings, and while he wasn't neglected, he did feel overlooked. A shy boy, Billy was small for his age and didn't mature as rapidly as his brother or peers at school. One day when he was fourteen, he walked in on his older brother having sex with his girlfriend. From that time on, Billy couldn't get the images out of his thoughts. Soon he began masturbating, imagining other people having sex, never picturing himself engaging in it. He was always the observer—the voyeur. In his unconscious mind, he had merged the episode with his brother with childhood feelings of invisibility and, from that crucible, created an erotic fantasy that brought pleasure to what had caused unhappiness and confusion. Now, as an adult, his sexuality was dependent on not being seen or actually participating in sex, a secret that kept him emotionally and sexually distant from Margot. That was, until they began speaking about it with my encouragement.

Instead of feeling threatened, Margot and Billy found the honesty of these conversations had sparked a sense of discovery and excitement. When Margot finally shared with Billy her fantasies of performing sexually for an audience of men, he laughed, rather than expressing outrage as she expected. He immediately confessed that he shared her fantasy and had been secretly imagining her with other men as a way of climaxing on the rare occasions they had sex. The conversations brought them emotionally closer, and soon they started discussing how they could act out their mutual fantasies safely. When Margot finally suggested they visit a sex club, Billy jumped at the idea, and together they searched the Internet. They decided on a club in another city because there would be less chance of running into anyone they knew. They planned a weekend away and agreed to a series of ground rules for how they would conduct themselves at the club, even creating a discreet "stop signal," a tug to the earlobe, to signal their discomfort with anything that happened.

Going to the sex club was enormously exciting, though not without anxiety. They were, after all, betraying the social conventions with which they were raised.

Checking their clothing at the door, they entered a room full of other couples engaged in various forms of sex. The freedom to be sexual in a public place, or in Billy's case to watch people being sexual, was immediately liberating and thrilling for both of them. With Billy's consent, Margot eventually joined in and, like Salome, teased and seduced a group of men and women. Amazingly, Billy felt no jealousy. In fact, he experienced Margot's behavior as an act of love and generosity, which turned him on sexually even more. No one had ever placed his needs first. In fact, his parents hadn't bothered to find out what he needed. For the first time in his life, he felt taken care of. Not only could he fulfill his voyeuristic longings while still partnered to Margot, but Margot also offered him the respect and generosity that had been missing in his life. He truly felt "seen." And he delighted in the knowledge that he could help her satisfy her own desires.

For weeks after, they discussed their feelings about the experience. The act of expressing their erotic fantasies by transgressing sexual conventions opened up conversations about trust, jealousy, rivalry, boundaries, and limits, further deepening the intimacy and bond between them. Where Margot had always felt controlled and disrespected by her mother, she now felt profoundly appreciated and respected by the person who mattered most in her life.

They dared to invent a life, regardless of the family and social rules with which they were raised, in which they acknowledged powerful longings and desires, giving pleasure to themselves and each other as well as depth and substance to the relationship.

• • •

Sometimes a couple may choose to refrain from acting out their fantasies if it is too far out of the comfort zone of one member, such as when one partner's fantasies involve the physical pain or humiliation of another, which is in conflict with that partner's erotic desires. In such cases boundaries can be drawn and a middle ground can be reached that both partners find exciting. Other times, the intimacy gained by openly discussing sexual differences can lead to surprising new sexual possibilities, as in the case of Sue and Tina.

ALYSSA'S CASE: LEAVING FANTASIES ALONE: SUE AND TINA

Sue and Tina came into therapy primarily to determine whether their sex life could be improved and, if not, how much it mattered. Sue, who had just turned twenty-eight, and Tina, thirty-two, met two years earlier through mutual friends and immediately hit it off. Tina had already built a successful business as an interior designer, and Sue worked part-time in retail and was attending school for graphic design. They quickly became close and within six months were living together. Like many couples, sex was hot for the first six to nine months of their relationship, but as the novelty wore off, sex had rapidly decreased in frequency and intensity. When they entered therapy, they had not been intimate in four months.

"Sue is just not that into sex anymore," Tina said with an edge of frustration in her voice. "She says that she just has a low sex drive. I don't really know what's changed. Things used to be really good in the bedroom. I love her and I want to make this work. But I am totally not okay with having a non-sexual relationship. I don't know what to do. We have talked about an open relationship, but as much as I want sex, I've tried that before and it really didn't work for me."

When I asked Sue about what had changed for her, she, too, was unsure. "I don't really know. I have never been that into sex. I want to make Tina happy. I understand her wanting to have sexual relationships with other people. She's not like me. But I am not totally cool with it. I think it would just push us further apart. So I do want us to start having sex again. But right now, I feel like it's more for her than for me. Honestly, I care more about the other stuff. Family and companionship. That stuff."

When I inquired about how Tina felt about this, she said that she was feeling deeply rejected. She thought that Sue's lack of interest in sex was because Sue just didn't feel attracted to her. Her attempts to initiate sex with Sue were regularly rejected, which had left her feeling sad and alone.

I talked in detail with them about the ideas behind intelligent lust and urged Sue and Tina to attempt the first steps on their own. Initially, I explained the work would be mostly personal, in which they could privately explore their individual desires and their origin. "But that ultimately the goal," I said, "would be to share what they had learned."

Tina wasted no time. She bought a journal and in it started to record her fantasies, things she thought about when masturbating, experiences she wanted to try, things she had done in the past that she found highly exciting. She described several short-term and two longer relationships, the more recent of which lasted five years and was with a woman whom she described as very "sex positive" but ultimately unavailable. She considered herself very sexually experienced, preferring the role of "butch top" with a more "fem" woman, but what became clearer through the "homework" was that she had a strong desire to dominate, even punish, her partner. She suspected having such desires for as long as she had been sexual, though she hadn't really allowed herself to fully acknowledge them, much less express them with a partner. "It's kind of threatening to think of myself that way," she said. "The only way I can imagine it is if I were in a relationship in which we both felt safe and it was playful."

When I inquired about her family life, she told me that she was the youngest of four and described her parents as "wealthy hippies." She realized she was attracted to girls at the age of twelve and started to sexually experiment with friends when she was thirteen. Her disclosure to her parents, at sixteen, was met with support, even celebration. Tina speculated that her desire to dominate might be a reaction to having had very few boundaries or structure in her childhood. "I never really felt anyone was in control. There was something free about that, but it didn't always feel safe," she said. "Sometimes I acted out just to see if there was some sort of consequence, but there never was. In my fantasies, I'm definitely in charge. I even enjoy tying my partner up and punishing her." She laughed. "Maybe I want to punish my parents."

Sue was obviously uncomfortable during my discussion with Tina and also had a much harder time with the assignment. She came to the session reporting that she had not yet had the time to start the work. Respecting her discomfort, I asked her if she thought that it might be helpful to come for an individual session in which we could explore the steps together. I offered the same to Tina, clarifying that they as a couple were my client and thus I would not keep secrets from either one of them, so the individual session was merely an opportunity to discuss aspects of each woman's sexuality that they might struggle to address while together at this time. These sessions might also, I explained, help us address any barriers either one of them might be encountering to doing this work.

While my meeting with Tina went smoothly and we more deeply explored her desires and their origin, Sue, when alone, struggled again to find the words to describe both her sexual history and her feelings about sex now. Over the course of the hour, however, she began to settle in to it and even seemed to find relief in talking. Sue described her household as restrictive in communication and affection and her parents as not afraid to slap or spank to reprimand their children. Her father was a drinker, and despite the family's Christian values, both she and her brother knew that their father was engaging in an affair. Their mother, when they tried to discuss this with her, immediately shut the conversation down in an accusatory fashion, and it was never brought up again. It was an unhappy and threatening childhood.

Sue described a much different experience than Tina had when she came to understand that she was interested romantically, not in men, as her parents dictated, but in women. Sue left home at sixteen and did not speak to her parents for three years. At nineteen, urged on by a therapist, Sue attempted to reengage with her parents and at this time told them that she was gay. Their outright rejection of her resulted in her continued detachment from her family. Her brother, with whom she had been close, also rejected her.

When I asked Sue about the details of her sexual history, she told me she often dated straight women or women who were already involved with a partner, thus making them ultimately unavailable and rejecting. I pointed out how these relationships seemed to echo her relationship with her parents.

Tina was Sue's first long-term partner and as such was her first opportunity to explore a sexual relationship beyond the usual "honeymoon phase" when the newness of a partner or the uncertainty of their attention was enough to sustain excitement. Tina was not rejecting Sue as others had. To the contrary, Tina was "hot" for her, which was a new experience and completely confused her. It soon became apparent to both of us that while rejection had seeped into every aspect of her life—she had even sought rejection out— her true desire, what she had eroticized in her earliest sexual and romantic fantasies, was being treasured in a way that she had never been. "Hot" for Sue was not being dominated, tied up, or punished; it was being cherished, adored, and loved.

In our next session together, we frankly discussed the differences in their sexual desires and the challenges it presented. Sue told Tina that Tina's fantasies frightened her because they were too much like her parents' treatment of her. "I get now that was the reason why I turned off to you. It's not because I'm not attracted to you. It's just too far out of my comfort zone."

Tina thanked her. "I didn't really understand that. It helps to know that."

Tina then took the opportunity to share with Sue more about herself—her history and the complexity of her desires. She explained that while she found the idea of dominating Sue hot, it wasn't all that she desired.

"There's a lot about you I love," Tina said. "I would love at some point to be able to experience some of my fantasies with you. And to not feel ashamed of my desires. I don't feel like there is anything wrong with them. But I get where you're coming from. And I care a lot more right now about being close with you than I do about just acting out my fantasies. It means a lot to me that you're even willing to talk about this stuff at all with me, and I'm willing to go slow with it."

Both women had relaxed by the end of this session. They agreed that it was the most intimate conversation they had ever had together and that they felt closer than they had in a long time.

At the next session, they said they had tried something completely different. It started with Tina giving Sue a massage, which allowed her to feel in charge and Sue to feel treasured. Other physical but mostly nonsexual touches followed. "For the first time," Tina said, "we really paid attention to each other's bodies. It was so relaxed and pleasurable."

Sue nodded her head in agreement.

Tina went on. "I don't know what will happen in the future, and it's not the hottest sex I've ever had, to be honest, but it's definitely pretty cool."

ALYSSA'S THOUGHTS
Monogamy

I think that most people, gay and straight alike, feel that having a lifelong partner is preferable to going through life alone or with a series of affairs or even serious shorter-term relationships. What many tell me is that that life would feel too self-involved without a partner, even in light of the pain and conflict that might occur over the course of a long-term relationship. In fact, they say, working through these struggles contributes to life's meaning and purpose. For this group, monogamy is not only a desire, but also considered a necessary condition of the relationship—a means of protecting its stability and sustainability.

I also see in my practice other men and women who are openly exploring alternatives to monogamy. Some younger clients are even trying out polyamory. These folks are asking questions such as "Is long-term commitment a desirable goal?" and "Is it preferable to go through life coupled to the same person, or is it equally enriching to have multiple partners whatever the duration of the relationships?" Many of these young people have been raised in families in which their parents' marriages have failed or in which they experienced their parents as hopelessly entrapped. They fear duplicating what they perceive as rigid models of relationships and are instead experimenting with alternatives. Many have participated in or witnessed how the gay community is reinventing ideas about sexuality and partnership outside of marriage, including the creation of families of choice. The result is a more fluid view of what a significant relationship can be.

What is different, perhaps revolutionary, about intelligent lust is that it encourages people to understand and explore their sexuality honestly, openly, and responsibly without presuppositions. Out of this process, monogamy becomes a choice based on what is right for the individuals involved, a choice to be seriously discussed and evaluated rather than followed as a prescription of religious and social norms or some assumed or unspoken rule.

My opinion is that a restorative relationship, as described in this book, has many advantages. It provides the opportunity for partners to fully explore their sexuality over time. Certainly these relationships have their challenges, even when they are founded on generosity and respect. I think the trick to their long-term success is in maintaining an ongoing conversation about sex even when it's difficult, such as when we feel sexually interested in people other than our partners. When these feelings do occur, we must acknowledge them to each other and make an intelligent decision about what to do rather than keeping them secret or sweeping the issue under the carpet. It's secrecy that usually threatens relationships. I think monogamy does not necessarily improve the chances of a relationship's survival; it's the ongoing conversation about our feelings and the freedom to reexamine choices that makes the difference. Keeping the truth hidden can be subversive.

The steps of intelligent lust help us cultivate the self-esteem and confidence to acknowledge such truths. Guiding my clients through the steps gives them the information they need to make relevant and meaningful choices about their lives. Knowledge is power. Rather than dividing a couple, discovering and sharing knowledge will lead to greater intimacy and understanding.

In my work, I do my best not to impose my beliefs or preference on clients. As individuals, I think we should consider all the possibilities open to us, weigh the consequences, and make the choices that promote the greatest growth and health for all concerned. Nothing should be assumed or taken for granted. You read earlier in the book about some of the choices that couples made when they encountered differences in their sexual preferences that could ultimately have divided them. You can follow their solutions or invent your own. Freud said that marriage was both a "prison and a refuge." I think the constant element of choice helps keep marriage from imprisoning us.

CHAPTER 11

The Advantage of Sex

S ex is an affirmation of life. By making sex a prominent part of it—placing it on the top of our list of priorities—it helps us face daily challenges in other parts of our lives. No matter what struggles there are, we put them aside and establish a time and place to embrace desire and pleasure. We are less likely to fight over folding the laundry or the details of renovating the house when we feel sexually satisfied. By following the steps of intelligent lust, we cultivate a physical and emotional language that allows our deepest emotions to be expressed and understood, constantly injecting new vitality into our relationship and increasing the quality of our lives together. Smart sex is better than great sex because it leads to building a relationship in which our sexual desires can be used to heal childhood conflicts and satisfy unmet needs that we have carried into adulthood. Communication, respect, trust, and generosity that begin in the bedroom find their way into every aspect of the relationship. Intelligent lust gives us an advantage in dealing with life.

Relationships that grow out of this process are stronger than those based on other factors such as social standing, security, or similarities in backgrounds and religion. Many of those so-called well-matched relationships fail because sex and sexual compatibility have not been a priority, and the relationship lacks that connection and all the ingredients that go into making it.

Whether it's because of self-denial, poor communication, or misunderstanding of our true desires, problems arise in the relationships when thoughts and feelings go unspoken and resentments and frustrations build. When a relationship lacks the restorative elements of self-acceptance, transparency, and authenticity gained by following the steps of intelligent lust, there is often self-serving, abusive, or manipulative behavior taking place instead.

Typically when this occurs, men are more likely to express their frustrations by acting them out by drinking or engaging in secret affairs than they are by inviting discussion. We've all heard the refrain—"Men think with their dicks, not with their brains." For women, conversation usually comes first. But after a few attempts fail, their behavior usually grows more covert, using criticism to undermine a partner's self-esteem or playing the victim or martyr in an attempt to gain sympathy or, in some cases, living in a state of silent contempt.

On the other hand, in relationships in which smart sex is the centerpiece, behaviors like overreacting, acting out, or passive-aggression are less likely to occur. And a secret affair doesn't typically happen when people are continuously communicating about their needs, sexual and otherwise.

The fact is that we are all driven by the same insecurities and frustrations. It's not that "men are pigs" or "women are selfish bitches"; it's that those relationships that favor secrecy over transparency, pretense over authenticity, detachment over intimacy, ritual over exploration, are much more vulnerable to trouble. Relationships are systems in which problems grow out of the interactions of everyone involved. "Bad" behavior doesn't happen as an isolated act. Scratch the surface of the relationship and you will discover a cycle of actions, reactions, and counteractions that lead to it.

Of course, new challenges occur over time for every couple. Their resolutions require a process of direct communication, understanding, and problem solving. Couples who have investigated their sexual and emotional connection by following the principles of intelligent lust have already proven their ability to handle difficult and sensitive issues.

Margaret and Frank faced such a challenge.

FAITH THROUGH SEX: MARGARET AND FRANK

Frank's father, a career military man who joined the army right out of high school, prided himself in his well-behaved children, an accomplishment he believed derived from strict military protocol. But Frank silently suffered throughout his childhood and adolescence. By the time he reached college, he had eroticized being a disciplinarian himself and became aroused by thoughts and images of administering punishment to his partners.

Margaret had grown up in a strict religious household in which sex was considered shameful. As a young woman, she felt guilty for having sexual thoughts, yet could not do anything to control them. In fact, whenever she heard her friends talking about sex, she was instantly aroused.

As we began to examine her sexual thoughts and fantasies during therapy, Margaret realized that what truly excited her was what she called "dirty talk." A well-adjusted middle-school teacher, she imagined men calling her sexual names and describing to her how they would engage her in a variety of sexual acts. For this, of course, she also felt guilty and believed she should be punished. With therapy, she came to accept and appreciate the purpose of these fantasies as she understood more about how she had eroticized childhood religious beliefs that she now felt had been unfairly imposed upon her.

During the dating phase of our work together, Margaret met Frank at a teacher's conference where he was making a presentation as the vice principal of a nearby school district. Over the course of several dates, Margaret talked openly with Frank about sex, during which time they recognized that their turn-ons were complementary. In time, they began to experiment by acting them out. They negotiated the terms of the initial sexual scene through conversation and boundary setting. Frank would talk dirty to Margaret, telling her about all the things he was going to do to her; this would arouse her tremendously.

Later in the scene, Frank would discipline her for behaving like a "naughty" girl, which would excite him tremendously as well. They repeated this scene regularly, each time changing the script, sometimes wearing costumes or uniforms, and often stretching the boundaries. These negotiations required enormous trust and respect, as well as a level of honesty and freedom that neither had ever imagined could be possible with anyone.

It was not only in sex that they related so well. The couple came to enjoy doing many things together outside the bedroom, where they learned to treat each other with the same respect that marked their sexual scenes.

As time went on and life presented them with the usual difficulties, the couple seemed able to navigate them with greater ease

than many of the other couples they knew. They had built a foundation for conversation and negotiation in which nothing was off-
limits. They could apply these skills to any problem.

Then a crisis occurred: a student accused Frank of soliciting her
for sex. He vigorously denied the charges to school officials—and
to Margaret—but despite his denial, he was placed on probation
until an investigation had been completed.

Margaret found the charges ridiculous. Not only did she believe
Frank's denials due to their mutual trust, the details of the girl's
accusations did not match up with what Margaret knew about
Frank's sexual preferences. For Margaret, the trust and respect that
she had nurtured with Frank, which started with sex, extended
way behind beyond the bedroom walls. By establishing sex as a
priority in their relationship, they continually explored the nuances
and subtleties of their desires with emotional honesty and, in the
process, cultivated a profound understanding of one another that
permeated every aspect of their lives.

While Frank was on probation, Margaret stood by him, defend-
ing him to friends and family against their judgments. Luckily, the
student eventually confessed to her mother that she had fabricated
the accusations to distract school officials from her failing grades.
The case was closed, and Frank was reappointed to his position.

OVER THE LONG-TERM

Intelligent lust isn't about immediate gratification.

As our experience matures, we discover the deeper subtleties and
nuances of our own and our partner's erotic truth. Over time, as past
conflicts heal, desires change too. Couples may find themselves less
interested in the kind of sex that once attracted them. Underneath

the sexual compatibility that originally drew the partners together, there are deep psychological and spiritual connections. And while the frequency or intensity of sex may decline or entirely disappear, the ability to handle life's complex emotions only increases with experience. Even if one partner changes at a different pace than the other, the standard of life we've fostered over the long-term, with its deep respect and trust, sustains us. We've established a life outside of the bedroom in which creativity and pleasure continues to hold a central place even when sex doesn't.

SHOCK TREATMENT: BARBARA AND GRETCHEN

When my patient Barbara started dating Gretchen during Barbara's last year of college, they were both political activists, members of the feminist caucus on campus. They were attracted to each other as much by their political beliefs as by their physical appearance and attitude. From their first date, Gretchen was generous with her praise and affection toward Barbara, which is exactly what Barbara had hoped for in a mate, having grown up with little of either as the only daughter among four competitive brothers.

By the time Barbara was fourteen, she recognized that she was "different" and that her attraction was to other girls. It never created much of a conflict for her. She simply accepted it as a natural expression of who she was and pursued her interests accordingly. What was more troubling to her, though, was that when she began to have sexual fantasies, she imagined herself as a delicate girl dressed in lace and frills. Barbara experienced herself as everything but delicate. Even as an adolescent, she was tall, thick, and muscular with a cocky attitude that mimicked her brothers. As she grew into adulthood, it became difficult for her to reconcile her fantasies with her feminist beliefs.

When she met Gretchen, she was electrified by her fierce intelligence and her forceful presence. When they became sexual after a few months of dating, they each felt that they had met their perfect match. Gretchen not only made up for the affection that Barbara missed during her childhood, but she was more powerful in bed, allowing Barbara to embrace her secret "girlie side," which, surrounded by four aggressive brothers, she had learned to conceal. "Survival," she told me in therapy, had depended on being as "tough and ballsy as they were."

For twenty years Barbara and Gretchen built a life together, Barbara as a social worker advocating for abused women, Gretchen as a documentary filmmaker. They created a family of close friends, many of whom, like them, applied their feminist beliefs in their work.

While they were active sexually in their early years, as time moved forward, sex gradually diminished. But because the relationship was loving and supportive and had allowed each of them to play out their fantasies to the fullest, it had gratified those unmet needs from childhood for which their desires had served as antidotes. Acting out their sexual preferences had allowed them to integrate aspects of themselves that their role in their original families hadn't permitted. Each grew to embrace the complexity of who they were. The relationship had been truly healing for both of them.

On the morning of September 11, 2001, Barbara was standing at the window of her and Gretchen's forty-eighth-floor apartment just five blocks from the World Trade Center, eating a bowl of her favorite cereal as she typically did before work. They had taken the apartment because the view of downtown was so sweeping. The Twin Towers stood as its centerpiece.

Out of the corner of her eye, she saw an airplane flying in the direction of the towers. Before she could even grasp what was happening, the plane flew into the tower and flames spread across her view. She dropped her breakfast to the floor, ran into the bedroom where Gretchen was asleep, woke her, and pulled open the shades.

"A plane crashed into the Trade Center," she sobbed. But before she could finish her sentence another plane was headed for the second tower. Gretchen jumped out of bed and the two watched as the second plane hit. They stood at the window embracing, tears running down their cheeks as victims chose their deaths by jumping from their office windows.

When the towers fell and debris struck their building, they were evacuated down the darkened stairway, forty-eight flights, by firemen and, in the chaos, left to wander the streets. Dazed and bereft, they walked slowly uptown, choking on the smoke and smell until they arrived on the Upper West Side at the home of a good friend.

Three weeks later they were allowed to return to their apartment, which was now coated in ash. With the aid of the Environmental Protection Agency, the apartment was restored to normal, but outside the window was a huge gaping hole where the towers once stood. Now a bright searchlight lit the space twenty-four hours a day.

After the initial shock wore off, Barbara and Gretchen had opposite emotional reactions to the event. Barbara cherished all that she had in her life and felt especially close to Gretchen and others whom she loved, wanting to draw them even nearer. Gretchen felt, "Life is short and I better make the most of it." While Barbara clung to Gretchen, wanting to spend precious time with her, Gretchen felt she "wanted to live in the moment." That included having sex again. The couple had long ago given up their sexual relationship, but now Gretchen demanded one. The difference in their reactions was what brought them to therapy.

After some history gathering during the initial session, we focused on the events of September 11, six months earlier, and each of their experiences of the grief that followed. While they had repeated the story many times to friends, they connected deeply to their emotions, reliving each moment as they had remembered it, but now, without the veil of shock. It was a profound and moving session.

In the next session we talked about how the attacks had changed their attitude toward life. Gretchen spoke movingly about how easily life could be cut short and how important it was to make each day "meaningful and satisfying." Barbara told about the "surge of love" she felt for Gretchen and her overwhelming desire to be in her presence. When Gretchen finally mentioned that sex was an important way to stay connected, Barbara said since neither of them seemed particularly interested in sex long before September 11, Gretchen's renewed desire came as a great surprise.

"It just isn't in my frame of reference anymore. I feel satisfied just being close to Gretchen, sleeping next her, holding her. I never felt our relationship was any less vital because we were no longer having sex."

Unlike many couples who come for therapy, there was an ease in their communication that was accompanied by open exchanges of tenderness and affection. Not only was it clear that they cared deeply for each other, but they also cared about what each other needed.

"I don't want to give up having sex for the rest of my life,"

Gretchen said poignantly. "September 11 reminded me that I was missing it. It made me think of what I value. Something we did well together."

Barbara nodded her head understandingly.

Previously, when I had tracked their sexual history, I had learned that early in their relationship they had gone through their own version of the steps of intelligent lust, which served as the foundation for a restorative relationship.

For Gretchen, sex became a way to counteract the powerlessness she felt as a child. Her parents were both "self-involved actors," who seemed to "perform the role of parents rather than actually being them." They were more like "shadows of people, and frankly they didn't know what do with me. I kind of raised myself. I did what I wanted, when I wanted because I could, and it wasn't always pretty." By adolescence, she had turned sexually promiscuous, dominant, and aggressive with other girls. In effect, she had eroticized the lack of power she felt in gaining her parents' attention and found it thrilling to discover a way to get others to respond to her. In college, she used that energy in her work as a social and political activist, rising to a leadership position for which she was highly respected on campus.

"When I met Barbara she was there, there! She was a real person and was really into me and that changed my life," Gretchen said lovingly. "She was as strong and powerful as I was, but really tender in bed." It became evident from our conversations that Barbara's admiration for Gretchen, as well as her obvious desire for her sexually, had satisfied both of their needs. They quickly discovered that they were sexually compatible. In bed, Barbara could liberate her most "girlie" self without fearing rejection. Gretchen could freely express her dominance and enjoy Barbara's femininity. Over time, they had many happy and playful moments, sometimes taking their "masculinity and femininity" to stereotypical extremes, often with humor.

As Gretchen's story unfolded, I began to wonder if the trauma surrounding September 11 had awakened feelings of powerlessness and confusion similar to those that had once dominated Gretchen's childhood but had since diminished through her loving partnership with Barbara.

Eventually I spoke. "Fear is such a primitive emotion. When we experience it as an adult, it triggers the emotional memories we have of it as a child. It's like a highly combustible chain reaction. We automatically mobilize those defenses that worked for us in the past to try to contain the fear we feel in the present. I wonder if that might be going on now with you, Gretchen. I don't mean to underestimate the importance of the idea of living in the moment or the importance of desire. But I have a feeling you're taking things a step further, or perhaps a step back, more accurately, to how you protected yourself as a young person when you felt alone, frightened, and powerless in your family. I remember your motto: 'I'll do what I want, when I want to.' And mostly that meant expressing your feelings sexually. You found strength as well as a way out of your loneliness by connecting sexually with other girls. I wouldn't be surprised if those same underlying feelings are driving your sense of sexual urgency now."

We sat in silence for what seemed like a long time but what was probably only a few minutes. Gretchen seemed to be taking in what I said. Her eyes began to well with tears. "I hadn't thought of it that way. It didn't occur to me." She paused again. "I am scared. And I do feel helpless. I haven't really let myself feel that since the day of the attack."

Barbara gently reached for Gretchen's hand. We sat in silence another few moments until Barbara spoke. "There's been a lot of pressure on me to have sex, but to be honest, it didn't feel like it was sex that you wanted. I was confused. I couldn't figure out what you needed and give it to you. Don't get me wrong. I'm not trying to get off the hook about having sex. I'm not against it. It's true that sex doesn't matter to me the way it once did, but I can get into it again if that's what you want. It's just that I really didn't feel that's what you were asking for."

Suddenly, a smile crossed Gretchen's face. She wiped her tears with her hand.

"Can we have sex just for the fun of it then?" She laughed.

Barbara laughed too. "I'm game," she said.

Barbara and Gretchen had always considered each other's needs. Over the years, they maintained a relationship that was respectful and supportive, that had deep roots in their early experiences of sexual exploration. And while in later years, they had silently agreed to a relationship in which sex didn't play a central role, Gretchen had raised the issue again in reaction to the fear aroused by the events surrounding September 11. As sometimes happens in therapy, a switch gets turned on. By recognizing the meaning she had placed on sex, Gretchen instantly felt free to handle it differently. The insight offered her a choice—a way to diffuse the heaviness and pressure she had placed on sex. She could deal with her current fear by discussing it with Barbara and uncouple it from the idea of renewing a sexual relationship. They could approach sex again without the sense of urgency. And from what I understand, they did.

ALYSSA'S THOUGHTS
Generosity

I think women of my father's generation may have a harder time with issues of shame and guilt since conventional ideas of sexual morality are so deeply entrenched in their history. On the other hand, I think they also have a greater understanding of the generosity required to create meaningful and satisfying relationships. Many men and women of my father's generation—that is, children of the 1960s—worked together in movements advocating for political and social causes, including civil rights, women's rights, or protesting the war in Vietnam. There was a strong feeling of being in something together to benefit society as a whole—a kind of mass restorative experience that is ingrained in the consciousness of their generation. And while my generation and the following ones may have advanced on the ladder of sexual freedom and perhaps feel less shame about sex, they also have less of an understanding of the power of working collectively—"there for the greater good go I."

I see a trend toward self-involvement in younger people rather than toward sharing and giving. Generosity seems to be an underappreciated concept among us, perhaps because we were the first generation to be truly indulged by parents who themselves rebelled against the restrictive upbringing of the 1950s. The feeling I get from my contemporaries is that life is more about "me" rather than "we."

I have been using the steps of intelligent lust in my practice for the past several years and find that they can serve as an antidote to this. Intelligent lust not only makes sex a priority, but it also encourages empathy and equality: the ability to identify with a partner's experience and give it as much legitimacy as our own. It fosters an understanding and respect for a partner's interests and preferences. It values generosity above self-indulgence, beginning when we first enter into a dialogue about sex with a partner and continuing through acting out a partner's fantasies. Intelligent lust has a very strong "we" factor. Not only is there the opportunity for each of us to heal our own past conflicts and satisfy our sexual and deeper needs, but we can also help a partner heal his or hers. This allows for both the element of fun and passion in sex as well as emotional attachment. I believe that while the steps of intelligent lust focus on self-exploration, the ultimate goal is sharing. And I have found that most partners are just as excited by discussing and acting out their partner's fantasies as their own. It creates a sense of total openness and reciprocity and in turn allows each partner to relax into the experience. And knowing that you are acting out your partner's desires, seeing them aroused, is often a great turn-on!

If we teach people about their sexuality early in their lives, they will have the tools to seek more authentic experiences right from the start. This should provide greater protection from blindly falling into relationships with partners with whom we are not sexually compatible and with whom sex grows empty, boring, or meaningless—a typical death knell to a relationship. Without a real understanding and respect for our unique sexuality, we are more likely to marry a partner for the wrong reason.

CHAPTER 12

When Enjoying Sex Seems beyond Your Control

S ometimes our issues feel overwhelming, and self-help pro-
grams like following the steps of intelligent lust can seem
daunting. However serious, our problems exist for reasons, and
when we understand their meaning and purpose, it will give us a
new perspective. We find compassion for ourselves in knowing
that our problems are actually solutions to some of life's most
difficult dilemmas.

A lack of sexual interest, for instance, allows us to avoid sex and
all the potential conflict it might bring. On the other hand, engaging in frequent anonymous sex permits us to live in a safe state of
detachment immune from the complications of an intimate relationship. Aggressive sex may be our way of handling feelings of
powerlessness, having ourselves been abused at an earlier time in
our lives. And sex while using alcohol or drugs may be the only
way we can let go and even consider having sex. When we figure
out the underlying conflicts from which our behavior originates,
we can do those things necessary to heal them. Our problems become more manageable.

If enjoying sex somehow seems beyond your reach for any of the reasons mentioned, read this chapter for advice before following the steps of intelligent lust. Take inspiration from the stories told here.

LOW SEXUAL INTEREST

When it comes to desire, levels of sexual interest vary among individuals in frequency and intensity. Studies also show that erotic urgency ebbs and flows over the life span. Around 30 percent of young and middle-aged men and women go through extended periods of feeling little or no desire for sex.

Sometimes the lack of sexual desire can be attributed to physical transitions such as menopause or postpartum phases that produce fluctuations in hormones or to diminishing levels of testosterone in men. Life stresses, such as financial or work pressures, a child's illness, or the quality of turbulence in our relationships, can also affect our interest in sex.. Powerful physiological or psychological factors, sometimes both, change our attitude toward sex and the level of our sexual interest.

The most common reasons for women's lowered sex drive are

- postpartum and breast-feeding
- the onset of menopause
- prescription medications such as antidepressants, birth control pills, or blood pressure medications
- excessive stress and anxiety
- body image issues such as weight gain
- anger and resentment
- thyroid deficiencies
- diabetes
- a history of sexual abuse

The top reasons for lowered sex drive in men include

- alcohol and illegal drugs
- prescription medications such as antidepressants and heart medications
- excessive stress and anxiety
- low testosterone
- fatigue
- desire to control or punish
- depression
- enlarged prostate
- a history of sexual abuse

Women may not be the only ones who suffer the effects of changing hormones. Hormone changes are a natural part of aging. It's not uncommon for men, as young as forty, to find getting an erection less automatic and sexual interest diminished. By the time a man reaches seventy, testosterone levels can be reduced by as much as 50 percent.

But even when we have a low sexual interest due to physical changes or a life crisis, there are things we can do to rekindle our sexual desire if we value the importance of sex and its healing power. We can learn to accept the changes and cultivate a sex life with opportunities for affirmation and satisfaction. Try the following things.

Give Yourself Permission to Have Sexual Pleasure
Often when our self-esteem is flagging, we feel undesirable or ugly or perhaps even undeserving of pleasure. Even so, we can give ourselves permission to enjoy sex despite the reasons that led us to lose interest. While sex may not feel like a priority, it's also an experience we should not deny ourselves because of its many heal-

ing effects. Once we break through and reengage in sex, it tends to build on itself.

Establish a "Free Zone" Specifically for Self-Pleasuring

Institute a regular time and place, regardless of how you feel, in which you tune everything else out and tune in to sex. Use self-stimulation to reconnect to your fantasies and desires. Once your interest returns, you can initiate sex with a partner.

Stop Worrying about How You Look

You can make an effort to relax and be kind to yourself by appreciating the deeper nature of sex rather than how you think you will appear.

Use Your Fantasies

Even if you have difficulty getting an erection or suffer from vaginal dryness or some other medical condition, you can search for ways to express yourself sexually that are satisfying now. Many possibilities exist for sex that do not involve intercourse. Nongenital sex such as sensual touching, verbal play, extended kissing, massage, wrestling, bondage, tantric sex, and many other imaginative forms of contact can be immensely gratifying. You can use erectile and vaginal difficulties as an opportunity to explore possibilities that you might not otherwise consider.

Talk with Your Partner

Initiate a conversation with your partner about your experience. Ask him to help jump-start your sexual relationship in a way that could potentially excite you. This can help create a context of loving support and cooperation. Your partner is likely to have withdrawn sexually in response to your lack of interest, and he may actually find such conversation thrilling.

DIFFERENT STROKES: PAUL AND MELISSA

My patient Paul is an older man who has been married three times; Melissa, twenty years younger, has never been married and tended to bounce from one relationship to the next. They met when fixed up by a friend, and they hit it off immediately.

In the past, both Paul and Melissa had dated perfectionists whom they felt a strong need to please based on similar child-hood experiences with equally demanding parents. Eventually, they always rebelled against their partners' demands, and all their relationships ended in failure—a common trait they discov-ered on their first date, and one they liked talking about, as now they had each found a partner whom they didn't feel the need to please as much as simply enjoy. As neither had many expecta-tions of the other, they felt no need to protest and in a short time grew quite close.

Not long into their relationship, Paul and Melissa came to me for couples counseling. They wanted their relationship to work out, but they were concerned because the sex hadn't been good. It quickly became clear that despite their ability to discuss almost anything, they hadn't been talking to each other about sex; they had only been fumbling around unhappily in bed. Over time, I took them through the steps, opening their minds to what they truly wanted from sex, investigating their fantasies, talking can-didly as much as they felt comfortable.

What they discovered was that, at age sixty-seven, Paul's sexual drive was a fraction of what it had been. He was growing to love

208

Melissa, but much of that came from her companionship and the close physical contact they both enjoyed.

Melissa, however, was still sexual. Because her fantasies often centered on being told what to do by an authoritarian man, the couple eventually developed a practice that satisfied both of them: In bed, Paul would hold Melissa and tell her exactly what she should do to reach orgasm on her own. Once she had, Melissa would take time to embrace and caress Paul, which pleased him immensely.

This might strike some people as an odd compromise, but it was anything but that to the couple, who could now not only talk about sex but also regularly embellish on the scene to make it uniquely theirs—and it made them very happy as well.

But what if there is no medical explanation or other life crisis that accounts for the lack of our sexual interest? What if we are simply the type of person who never had much of an interest in sex or rarely even fantasized about it?

Some experts say that fantasy doesn't play as vital a role in women's sexuality as in men's or that when it comes to desire men have more of it than women—women are more interested in the quality of the relationship than in sex. But these characteristics, if they do exist, are more informed by social attitudes than biology. We hold men and women to different standards—sexually active women are judged negatively, while men advance on the social ladder for performing as studs. If women fantasize less or act less interested in sex, it's because, in our culture, they are not afforded the same sexual entitlement as men. Despite the enormous gains the women's movement has achieved in the last thirty years, when it comes to sex, many women still believe it's their role to please rather than seek pleasure for themselves.

Some of us give up on sex without ever understanding the reasons why. We choose to live celibate lives, sometimes justifying them with spiritual explanations. If we follow the steps of intelligent lust, we can confront those attitudes and defenses that stand in the way of knowledge and dig deeper to discover the real meaning and purpose for the absence of sex in our lives. Whether we disown sex to protect ourselves from experiencing shame, consider it a temptation, or fear being out of control, we can enlighten ourselves with the truth and eventually open up to the genuine satisfaction that comes from connecting to our deeper selves and another person.

THE MEANING OF DREAMS: AARON

My patient Aaron, for example, insisted that he had no interest in sex. His friends even made fun of him at their bachelor parties, he told me with some pride, because he was "nonplussed" about the sexual partying that often went on. He was the only guy in his fraternity not distracted by sex, which he believed was why he earned straight As.

But that was not the reason he came for therapy. He was concerned because he often felt exhausted. Though he made sure he had eight hours' sleep most nights, most mornings he woke up "wrecked." Now a highly paid software engineer, he could hardly keep his eyes open during the day. It was as if he had no sleep at all. He wondered if therapy could help.

First, I referred him to a physician, who determined there was no medical reason for his physical exhaustion and was as puzzled as Aaron about why he would fall asleep at his desk or have no energy in the evenings. A change in diet and the addition of supplements made no significant difference, and he could not get up the energy to return to the gym for regular workouts.

I wondered if perhaps Aaron's sleep was made fitful by disturbing dreams, so during our second session, I asked him to describe in detail what typically happened during his sleeping hours.

"I don't know. I fall asleep pretty easily. I usually read until I'm groggy then I turn the light off. I'm dead out. The next thing I know it's morning. The alarm rings and I can't open my eyes. I hit the ten-minute snooze button and wake up when it goes off. I feel like I haven't slept at all."

"Do you wake up during the night?" I asked.

"If I do, I'm not aware of it."

"Do you remember dreaming at night?"

"That's weird too. I never remember dreaming but I know I must."

"How do you know?"

Aaron was silent for a moment.

"Because either I am jerking myself off in my sleep or I'm having wet dreams," he said with an embarrassed smile. "I'm sticky down there."

"So you may be having a whole other life when you're asleep," I said.

He laughed.

I went on. "Do you have sex or masturbate at other times?"

"Not really. I don't have much of a sex drive. My friends in college even laughed at me because I was never interested in sex."

"Well, apparently you are when you're sleeping."

We both laughed.

"Yeah, I wish I was there to enjoy it," he said, still laughing.

"Do you ever have sexual fantasies?"

"No, I really don't think about sex."

I thought for a few moments about Aaron's situation then made a suggestion. It seemed obvious he had so thoroughly repressed his sexual desires that whatever was truly exciting to him must have seemed so unthinkable that he could not allow it to surface to his consciousness. He so thoroughly cut himself off from his sexuality, that he expressed no interest in sex at all.

But how could we discover what was behind his amnesia? I told him I thought it might prove helpful if he could do some research. I suggested that each night for one week until we met again, he set his alarm for different times during the night with the idea of catching himself in the middle of a dream or fantasy. I asked him to keep a paper and pencil handy to record what he recalled when he awoke.

Aaron took the experiment seriously. He returned the next week carrying a black leather-bound journal, which he opened immediately to the first page.

"I'm going to read this to you. Nothing happened the first two nights. But on the third night, here's what I wrote: 'Thursday, 3 a.m.: Dream. Feet. Beautifully sculpted, deep arches, soft gentle smell, natural toenails. Kissing them, gently rubbing them, and massaging them. Hard-on. Lots of precum. I am incredibly excited.' Wait. There's more. 'Saturday, 3:30 a.m. I'm sucking toes. No body or face attached. Just feet. Beautiful toes. I'm really hard. I rub my cock against the sole of the feet and start to fuck them. They grab my cock.'"

We sat in silence for a moment.

"How do you feel about what you discovered?" I gently asked.

"A mixture of being freaked out—shame and relief. I mean, it wasn't a total shock to me. I remember having more than the usual interest in feet and shoes as a kid. I loved going to buy new shoes. I didn't know what it meant. But the whole feeling of the shoe store, watching people take their socks off, the smell, trying on shoes, measuring feet. I would drag my mother into any shoe store when we were out shopping. After a few times, she must have sensed something. She told me it was 'odd.' We stopped buying shoes in stores. She would order them for me from catalogs.

"I'd hide the catalogues under my bed and read them at night. I didn't know why. I didn't know it was erotic, but I just couldn't wait to look at them. I also felt really ashamed. Later, in high school, when I took gym class, I tried not to look at the other kids' feet. At first I couldn't resist, then after time and a lot of bargaining with God, I made myself stop thinking about it."

"You said you felt a combination of shame and relief."

"I feel like a freak. I'm turned on by feet. Not a pretty face or breasts. Feet. That's kind of humiliating."

"Why relief then?"

"I don't know. I think it's because at least I'm sexual. I think I was already feeling like a freak because I had no interest in sex like every other guy in his twenties did. I wouldn't let myself think about sex at all. I didn't date or watch porn with my frat brothers. I just couldn't take the chance. I didn't want it to be true. But it's true. I'm turned on by feet. I don't know; it's confusing. What happened to that sweet little kid who just so happened to love feet? It's so sad."

Aaron began to cry. I waited until he calmed himself and then told him stories of other patients and their true erotic desires—the young man who got excited whenever someone sneezed, the rabbi and Kabbalah scholar who masturbated while thinking about women wearing eyeglasses. I talked about how our erotic desires had meaning and how we could together discover the poetry in the purpose of his fantasies. "Repression is a powerful defense against shame," I said. "In our attempts to protect ourselves against the unthinkable, it can cast a long, dark shadow over our lives, blanketing out large segments of who we truly are." His passion for feet was a "gift that deserved to be gently unwrapped, admired, and understood." I told him many people shared his appreciation, and at some point, he would discover them.

I explained the steps of intelligent lust and asked him to take the journey with me.

Compulsive Lust

While the principles of intelligent lust honor desire, they do not deny the dark and difficult aspects of it. Sex can be compulsive when we repeatedly pursue encounters with the hope that each new experience will relieve our tension, anxiety, or boredom or help us escape from pain or conflict. Because our body produces a surge of powerful chemicals during the excitement of sex, bingeing acts as a momentary antidepressant, blotting out pain and flooding us with feelings of well-being. But when the effect begins to wear off, we are left with even greater anxiety, feelings of emptiness, or shame from which we also crave to escape. The thought and pursuit of sex progressively dominates our lives until we are caught up in a cycle of compulsive lust or romantic obsession.

Every compulsion has a healthy intention—we enact rituals in an effort to soothe pain or conflicts—but the anarchy of compulsive lust leads to meaningless or reckless sex, or sometimes its opposite, sexual self-starvation. Without making a conscious attempt to understand the true nature of our sexuality, we cannot direct our energy toward healing. Compulsive acting out indulges selfishness and self-loathing, where intelligent lust generates self-love and generosity.

Compulsive lust can take many forms. Check your own behavior against the most common listed below:

- Frequent masturbation to relieve tension
- Cruising Internet sites regularly and losing track of time
- Constant use of pornography
- Multiple affairs
- Unsafe sex
- Multiple anonymous sexual partners
- Regularly patronizing prostitutes
- Unusually high drive
- Engaging in sexual activities that are against the law
- Constantly thinking about sex
- Secrecy or self-deception regarding sex
- Lying
- Never having sex with another person
- Only engaging in self-stimulation
- Using sex as a solution to other things
- Thinking about stopping but never getting there (you often try, but fail)
- Having sex is a priority over friends, family, or work
- A preoccupation with avoiding sex
- Feeling controlled by your sexual desire

DANCING WITH MEMORIES: ANITA

Like many young ballet dancers, Anita dedicated herself to her art with extraordinary focus and discipline, even to the exclusion of enjoying a typical adolescent social life. She had no interest in boys other than as partners in the ballets she performed.

Her talent and persistence paid off. She was invited to join the corps de ballet of a major New York City company when she was barely eighteen. In her first years there, she worked hard and earned the respect of her colleagues as well as the attention of the artistic director.

One evening, while performing the "shades" passage of the classical ballet *La Bayadère*, Anita collapsed on stage.

"My body gave out. I just couldn't move. I felt like I was going to die."

The collapse was attributed to exhaustion by the company physician, and although she recovered quickly, within a few months it happened a second time and then a third. The doctor placed her on leave and recommended rest and "fun."

During this time she suffered bouts of anxiety and depression, though she had no deeper explanation for them other than her immediate disappointment with herself for having been instructed to take time off. Her physical symptoms also continued. At times she was unable to move her body enough to get out of bed. Then she began to have disturbing dreams of violent sex in which she was tied up and raped. Specialists could find no reason for her physical symptoms. Suspicious that they may be psychosomatic, her doctor recommended psychotherapy.

By the time Anita came for a consultation, she was already beginning to remember what had happened to her as a small child, though the memories were vague and foggy, like faded photographs. Slowly, we reconstructed her history, and, as she directed her attention to these recent unsettling images, the words and story came into her memory too.

Much to her horror, she remembered that at around the age of six, while visiting her mother's sister in Wyoming, she was left in the care of teenage cousins while the adults attended a family wedding. During their absence, she was taken to the basement by her cousin, tied and bound, and repeatedly raped. He threatened to seriously hurt her if she repeated the story.

Because of her self-doubts about the event, a common stage in recovering traumatic memories, I helped her recount the story several times over the weeks that followed, each time filling in the details and supporting her in experiencing the emotions and the bodily sensations of the trauma.

Ballet had kept her at a safe distance from these memories. The strict discipline of her training gave her the feeling of having control of her body, while the intensity and focus of the dance distracted her from reexperiencing the emotional and bodily effects of the rape. Her separation from boys, except as ballet partners in which their activities were rigidly prescribed, also allowed her to keep them at a safe distance. And ballet was an art form that required her to remain mute. Perfect.

At times, we all have the experience of losing ourselves while watching a good play or movie, or reading a good book. But Anita dissociated: the memory of her trauma, along with all sexual fantasy and desire, were involuntarily erased from her consciousness. But even though the events were forgotten, the feelings associated with them had a long-term effect. The aftershock reached into adulthood before her body finally betrayed her. She developed debilitating physical symptoms that metaphorically revealed her secret—she became unable to move, similarly tied and bound as she had been during the rape.

• • •

Whether we suffer a gentle seduction or violent rape like Anita, the symptoms of post-traumatic stress can turn every aspect of our lives inside out. Some survivors feel guilty, even responsible, and often avoid sex entirely or continually reenact the trauma through sexually compulsive behavior. While most victims don't become abusers, some do eroticize the role of the perpetrator and act out their aggression by engaging in abusive sex. Men with histories of child abuse are more likely than women to imitate the perpetrator, transforming feelings of fear into power.

The most common symptoms of abuse include

- extreme states of mistrust, fear, depression, anxiety, or despair
- sexually compulsive behavior
- inability to get aroused
- erectile dysfunction
- feelings of detachment during sex
- flashbacks or disturbing fantasies
- vaginal pain
- considering sex an obligation
- avoiding sex

My patient Jennifer knew exactly what excited her. It wasn't something she gave much thought' she simply acted it out. Jennifer was always attracted to risk and danger and never wanted to know why or what her preferences meant. "That would have spoiled the thrill," she told me in hindsight.

By the time Jennifer came to therapy, she had already admitted that her sexual activities had grown beyond her control. The fact that she was married with two children hadn't stopped her from secretly seeking sex with strangers. But when she found herself obsessively thinking about prostitution, she finally decided it was time to look for help. Until that point, her personal life had been geared around how and with whom she would next have sex. As soon as she finished one encounter, she was thinking about the next.

And surprisingly, no one suspected.

"I was already having sex with strangers, why not get paid for it? That's how out of control I got," Jennifer said, describing her logic. "I finally realized that this has got to end. Is this what I want my life to amount to? I'm a thirty-five-year-old whore cheating on my husband. I couldn't even let myself think about the kids. I was constantly afraid of being caught. That's when I made the decision to stop."

A year before she came for therapy, Jennifer had gone on the Internet and found a Sexual Compulsives Anonymous group that met during the afternoons when her husband was at work and she was her most vulnerable. She began attending meetings several times a week.

After a few months, with the support of her group, Jennifer made the decision to come clean with her husband. She felt she had to take responsibility for her behavior—she had a moral obligation to tell him. And she no longer wanted to live in hiding. It was also the first time in her life that she had ever taken herself so seriously.

Her husband was both blindsided and devastated. He had no idea that Jennifer had a double life. He felt angry and betrayed. At first, he asked her to move out of the house, but not wanting to disrupt the children's lives, he settled for her sleeping in the guest room. He refused to move out of their bed, and he refused to speak to her unless it was about the children.

"I'll never forget the look on Michael's face. He was broken," she said, her own face as white as ash.

Somehow they survived the next six months. Jennifer faithfully attended SCA meetings. For the first time, she stopped keeping secrets, and along with deep feelings of shame, she also felt a sense of relief.

It had been an extraordinarily painful year for both her and Michael. Yet on the one-year anniversary of her sexual sobriety, to her surprise, Michael told her that though he would never forget the pain she caused him, he admired her determination to live a healthy life. He said he didn't know if he could ever fully trust her again, but he wanted to try. They both wept, and for the first time since her disclosure, they slept in the same bed.

But the more things improved with Michael, the more inexplicably sad she felt. She made another decision: to come to therapy to "finally face all the demons." When I asked her what that meant to her, she bowed her head and looked directly at the floor. After a few moments of silence, she began her devastating story, which she had told only one time before.

Jennifer and her two younger brothers were raised in a middle-class suburb of Detroit by her mother and stepfather. Her parents had divorced when she was six, and within a year her mother re-married her high school sweetheart and her father's best friend. Jennifer was nine when, while watching television on the living room couch—her mother out working the night-shift—her step-father asked her to massage his shoulder, which he said he had injured at work that day. He had asked her before, but always in her mother's presence. She always took pleasure in the idea of pleasing him, and with her brothers sitting nearby, she thought nothing of it.

Later that evening, after her brothers were in their beds and she in her own, her stepfather came to her room to thank her. He sat on the edge of her bed, brushed her hair with his hand, and gently kissed her on the cheek. Then, he placed his lips on her mouth and kissed her again. Though he left her room immediately after, in that instant her life changed.

Several nights later he returned to her room and instructed her to massage his chest. He removed his shirt and asked her to rub the lotion he had brought with him across his body. Within a short time, he pushed her small hand toward his penis and held it there.

His nighttime visits continued regularly, and soon he was placing her face down on her bed, taking her clothes off, and rubbing his body against hers, until one night he raped her.

"I was terrified. I never said a word. He told me that if I told anyone that he would tell them that I had made it up. No one would believe me."

The rapes went on for several years, sometimes more than once a week. Finally, on the day of her thirteenth birthday, she gathered her courage and told her mother that her stepfather was having sex with her. Her mother was shocked and devastated. Without hesitation, she called the police, and when her husband returned from work, he was confronted and arrested. The marriage ended right then.

Like most abuse victims, Jennifer felt it was impossible to make sense of all the feelings—anger, shame, guilt, love, pain, and fear—that occurred during and after that experience. As she entered puberty and developed physically, she became even more confused. Now she had sexual feelings, but along with them, associations that frightened her—she could not stop fantasizing about her stepfather. She imagined having vaginal intercourse with him, a thought which she found both horrifying and pleasurable.

By the time she was sixteen, she was regularly having sex with older boys and men. She felt powerful knowing she could please them. She was struggling to gain control over the pain and indignity by unconsciously acting out a more pleasurable version of her abuse. But because the meaning and purpose of her fantasies and behavior were not part of her consciousness, they could not produce true healing. Instead, compulsively acting out sex produced a numbing, narcotic-like effect that, for a time, served its purpose.

Now, twenty years after her abuse ended, she was finally dealing with those feelings rather than escaping from them. As we discussed the details of her trauma in therapy, she recognized that her childhood was stolen from her and could never be replaced. Soon she plunged into a period of genuine grief. Never before had she felt safe enough to allow such feelings, and now that she had, she didn't think she would ever stop feeling sad.

I invited Michael to the next session because I felt that providing a context for understanding her experience might open his heart and at the very least foster compassion. I was right.

As the deepest mourning lifted, anger replaced it. She began having fantasies of getting even with her stepfather. At the time of his arrest, her mother had been advised not to prosecute her husband because the events surrounding a trial would further traumatize Jennifer. Now Jennifer felt outraged and wanted to punish him.

During this stage, Michael and I bore witness to her story. Along with her SCA group, we supported her through each twist and turn of her grief over the period of a year.

The restorative powers of mourning are extraordinary. When the process is fully embraced, it runs its course and leaves room for a new perspective. And while life's challenges can reawaken some aspect of the trauma, its effects grows less powerful with time. Eventually the pain is left in the past and the task of rebuilding life in the present takes priority. Jennifer's courage paid off. She is finally prepared to follow the steps of intelligent lust and establish a sexuality that is separate and free from the trauma.

Before attempting the steps of intelligent lust, victims of sexual abuse should seek the support of a self-help group, physician, or mental health professional. We need first to fully understand what happened to us and the erroneous beliefs about ourselves that we may have assumed as a result. We are not "damaged goods" or "bad" or a "sexual object," as we may have come to think. We need to stop sexual behavior that reinforces the trauma, such as risky sex, sex we don't really want, and compulsive sex. We need to become conscious of our automatic reactions and identify when we are projecting or having a flashback, separating the past from the present. We need to do our best to identify those fantasies related to the trauma and allow ourselves to discover new desires. And not the least, we need to learn how to be touched and touch again outside of the associations of the past.

ALCOHOL AND SEX

A candlelit dinner with a glass or two of wine or a cocktail can set the stage for a romantic sexual interlude. The alcohol loosens inhibitions and makes it far easier to make the first move or to relax and surrender to an advance. But alcohol used in excess can cloud judgment and allow one to make poor decisions. Over time the effects of alcohol use on sex can be severe both psychologically and physiologically, including erectile dysfunction, suppressed interest, difficulty with orgasm, vaginal tightness, and much more.

While a small amount of alcohol might lubricate a conversation, too much of it disconnects us from deeper thoughts and feelings, dulling us in a way that doesn't allow access to the core of who we are. Instead of fostering intimacy, as we imagine, it keeps us at a distance from our true selves and our partner. That's often why people drink. Their guilt or shame about sex needs to be deadened before they can actually have it.

Excessive alcohol use interferes with our capacity to follow the principles of intelligent lust, in which we want to know what we really feel about sex and use those feelings to guide our behavior (the symptoms of alcohol abuse can easily be found online). Consulting a substance abuse counselor or attending a twelve-step program may be necessary before attempting the steps of intelligent lust. Even with support, if sex has been closely associated with alcohol, investigating our deepest thoughts and fantasies, is likely to raise powerful feelings that we have long denied or avoided, and that can threaten sobriety.

My patients, John and Cindy, came together at a particularly vulnerable moment in both their lives. From our telephone conversation days earlier, I knew that John and Cindy were both recovering alcoholics. I also learned that John, forty-five, was older than Cindy by almost fifteen years. Cindy was studying for a doctoral degree in education, and John, an art consultant, had a great deal of pride in Cindy's accomplishments. They lived together, though not married, in Hell's Kitchen, a mid-town Manhattan community that had been greatly gentrified in recent years. John earned a good salary, enough to support them comfortably even after the economic downturn.

In dress, each partner remained faithful to his or her age and vision of him- or herself. John, trim and fit at six feet, wore a dark blazer, blue button-downed business shirt, and a dark tie. Cindy, also tall and with fine angular features, was at once conventional and elegant, in a black skirt, high leather boots, and white silk blouse with a colorful Hermes scarf, which added a youthful flair.

When I asked, during our initial session, the standard question about why they had sought an appointment with me, they said the fear of violence had inspired them.

Violence. Nothing about either one's demeanor had suggested that there could be a violent moment between them, but Cindy confessed that there had been an incident of violence that was quite frightening to both of them.

I asked for a detailed account, and Cindy began to speak, her tone shaped by a slightly embarrassed edge.

"I overreacted," she said, then fell silent.

John looked at her with compassion.

"What happened was I reached up and placed my hand against the back of Cindy's head and gave her neck the slightest squeeze. Her response was so exaggerated."

"You surprised me," Cindy said.

"Maybe that was the extra ingredient—that I surprised her. I'm not exactly a touchy-feely person, but occasionally I do like to express my affection. I know she is sensitive to being touched. But it was our anniversary. Two years. And I just felt like acknowledging it."

"What happened next?" I asked.

"It struck me the wrong way. I didn't want to be touched like that. I felt violated. I lost control and punched him." A look of deeper embarrassment crossed her face.

Why had a loving gesture gone so wrong? Had John unwittingly transgressed a forbidden boundary, or was Cindy's reaction simply an anomaly?

I asked if there were other moments of violence between them.

"No, never," Cindy answered.

"So there have been times when you do touch and it's comfortable?" I asked.

John answered. "Yes, sometimes. It's usually when she initiates it. I've learned not to start anything. I'm generally very respectful of her space. This was the first time anything like this happened. It frightened us both."

"It felt sexual to me, and I was just not in that place," Cindy added.

I nodded my head in acknowledgment.

"We don't have sex very often," John said, then hesitated. "We're just not that sexual. I'm sure it came out of left field, and I'm sorry for that. Sex really isn't that important to me—to us right now."

Cindy picked up the conversation.

"We both kind of agree about that. It's not that I'm not into John. I think he's very attractive, but I have a lot of work to do on myself right now. Staying sober is a lot for me to handle. I love John. I think he's an amazing man. Kind and supportive. The list of things I like about him is endless. I feel close to him. We're really good together," she said emphatically.

John's face fell into a smile. "I feel close to you too."

I asked them how they first met. They answered that they had first spoken to each other at a meeting of Alcoholics Anonymous. They had seen each other at several meetings before. Eventually, John approached Cindy and struck up a conversation. They became friendly at subsequent meetings and even sat together. They seemed proud of their slow and deliberate speed in striking up a relationship. They made every move according to the highest AA standards.

They talked about "the program" and how grateful they were for its existence, and for the dedication and generosity of its members. John had been sober six years, Cindy for three.

During their animated testimony about AA, I marveled at how respectful they were of each other, pausing to let the other speak. It seemed like a dance of caution played out in the most friendly and mannerly way but in such contrast to the violence that had erupted on the second anniversary of their meeting.

As we drew near to the end of our first session, I considered the information that I learned. They seemed to demonstrate an enormous amount of respect for the other person's personal and intimate territory. While each had expressed a feeling of closeness, they were also remarkable in maintaining a comfortable distance. Even their body language suggested restraint.

I told them admiringly, "I've been watching and listening as each of you demonstrates an enormous amount of respect for the other's personal space. You seem to have figured out a level of intimacy that serves you both well for the moment—an exquisite balance between closeness and distance. Too intimate a connection might threaten the personal boundaries you're building with the assistance of AA. My suspicion is that you each fear that sex might disturb those boundaries and consequently your sobriety." They both nodded their heads in acknowledgment. I went on.

"Although none of us condones violence, I can understand how the episode you described might have protected you from this potential threat. It was, after all, your anniversary—a day of celebration of your togetherness. I know this is going to sound strange, but a simple act of violence may have protected you from any further temptation of togetherness—from tipping the balance of closeness on such a special day. The way you touched Cindy was an invitation to have sex and consequently a challenge to your mutual agreement to leave sex out of the equation of your lives for now in order to achieve a higher purpose. It's ironic, but violence may have been the anniversary gift Cindy gave to herself and to you. She reminded you, as severe as it was, that sobriety comes first and that's best protected by keeping the right distance."

An expression of relief passed over their faces.

I noticed right away at the beginning of the second session, a week later, that their mood had altered slightly. They seemed more unsettled.

A moment barely passed when Cindy confessed that she was battling the urge to have a drink. Sinking deeper into the soft sofa, she said she was struggling more than usual to protect her sobriety. She was working the program, attending meetings daily.

I wondered if our first session had eased the shame and anxiety caused by the touching/hitting episode and allowed the atmosphere to calm. Could it be, as I had suspected, that too much warmth could unsettle them?

I decided to move backward in time, to tap a deeper vein of comprehensibility. I wanted to understand what they were protecting themselves from and at what sacrifice. As if in an AA meeting, I asked each of them to tell his or her story.

Cindy, speaking first, volunteered that her father was an active alcoholic, given to violent episodes. She said the family's attempts to avoid her father's rages long ago became a centerpiece of family life, much of which was organized around either not upsetting her father or getting away from him when he was drinking. Her mother was consumed with her husband's drinking, allowing very little attention for Cindy and her siblings.

Cindy said she escaped by fleeing into academic interests, which served her very well. The extra ingredient of total dedication helped her get accepted on scholarship to Harvard, an achievement that otherwise would have been unattainable because of the family's economic situation. She excelled at first, but the pressure of the scholarship and maintaining a part-time job began to get to her. She felt awkward among the other students and worried how she could hold up educationally and socially against those who had gone to selective schools and came from privileged families. She moved around campus as if she were on stage and the other students were finding her performance lacking. She began to drink to ease the pressure.

In her second year, Cindy plunged headlong into heavy drinking. In a relatively short time, she had progressed from binge drinking to daily marathons. She also began having sex indiscriminately. Blackouts followed in which she often forgot how she had gotten herself into a sexual situation. To protect herself, she holed up in her room and stopped attending classes.

Reports of her behavior and subsequent fights over it with her mother and siblings resulted in near total alienation from her family. Eventually, she fell so far behind in her academic work that she was forced to drop out of school.

But the drinking and self-loathing didn't stop. She described herself as "seething with rage" toward her father, ironically for his alcoholism and rage. In the combined rage and stupor, swathed in self-pity and shame as well, she said she "hit bottom." A man she randomly met at a bar and slept with convinced her to attend an AA meeting. She ended her story by saying that this act of rescue, plus several that followed it when she slipped back into the bottle during her introduction to recovery, had saved her life.

She finished her testimony with less emotional tension than when she had begun.

John, who had been watching with compassion as Cindy chronicled her descent and ascent, picked up his cue and talked about his background growing up as the son of successful parents, both corporate attorneys with homes in New York and Florida. His parents were very active socially, traveling frequently and, when at home, hosting many "fabulous" parties lubricated by alcohol. While given all of the material best, John was essentially left to grow up on his own, his parents demonstrating more interest in their work and each other than in him. At an early age, John discovered he was gifted as a pianist, and as he grew into a young man he excelled. He got invited into the "best homes" where people fawned over his playing, often rewarding him with cocktails or after-dinner drinks lasting late into the night.

For John, alcohol was more seductive. He did not turn to it to escape part of his life; it was part of life, every day. Bloody Marys and mimosas replaced morning coffee on weekends; wine washed down every meal after breakfast; and no sound lifted the late-afternoon, summer doldrums like the tinkling of ice cubes crashing against the walls of a crystal vessel. Drinking was not associated with violence or escape for John, quite the contrary. Alcohol escorted *fun* to every gathering. Sex was often part of the fun too.

Unlike Cindy, John felt little anger and no real pressing motivation to quit drinking or even confront the possibility that it might be a problem, until the accident occurred. Driving home from a party one evening with a few friends as passengers, John lost control of his car and crashed headfirst into a tree. While the passengers luckily suffered only minor injuries, both of John's arms were broken as well as his nose and most of his teeth.

The accident brought into focus an obligation to take care of himself or perish. No one brought John to an AA meeting; he decided to find one himself.

I now understood from their narratives that stability had no roots in either of their histories. They had in common a chaotic childhood marked by a lack of parental love.

As I braided their stories together in my mind, I tried to imagine what each must have felt before their lives dissolved into a hopeless fog of drinking. I sat in wonderment over what they had achieved in recent years, individually and with each other—*stability*—with its unfamiliar consistency and serenity.

I struggled to find the language to describe what I was thinking and to express the respect that I felt for their courage and discipline.

"It's amazing how far you've each come independently in the past few years and also how much you've accomplished together. Two years of relative serenity coupled with feelings of closeness. I understand now that these are feelings that neither of you had experienced before." They shook their heads again.

"You've taken incredible leaps in becoming sober, including separating from your families. You chose each other—you're both very different from each other's family members. How? Both of you are interested in and respectful of the other's needs, something none of your parents seemed to succeed at. You are also genuinely kind and loving to one another, experiences that seem to have been absent in your former lives. And that's not all. Within that affection, you've established a degree of intimacy that also helps you maintain your sobriety—neither too close nor too distant.

"You've come together to form a beautiful and generous bond, a restorative relationship, in which each of you is helping the other repair your past."

I paused until I felt the information had settled. Soon John reached for Cindy's hand. They both smiled.

These few sessions affected them profoundly. It seemed to push them into a different plane of perception as well as a deep appreciation for what they had each accomplished in the service of the other.

"I think the struggle for you now is about how to go further—how to bring new things into your life while maintaining your sobriety. This," I said, "is an important part of recovery.

"For instance, sex. Both of you have sacrificed something so fundamental to living fully by not daring to express yourselves physically. You both must see physical affection as a stepping-stone to sex, and sex for both of you has been dangerously inseparable from alcohol. One has acted as a trigger for the other. Because, in the past, you were both intoxicated when you had sex, neither of you probably have any real understanding of what your true desires are."

"That's true," Cindy said. "I think we both had a lot of the wrong kind of sex. I'm totally scared and confused by sex. Add guilt and shame to those feelings too."

"I don't know where to begin. How do we have sex without drinking?" John asked.

"When you both feel ready, we can work together on introducing sex into your lives. Talk about it at home. I think you'll know when the time is right."

A month after that session, they called to say they were ready to examine who they were sexually. And so when they returned, we cautiously set out together to follow the steps of intelligent lust.

ALYSSA'S THOUGHTS
Premature Ejaculation

Among the most common concerns for which a man will seek sexual therapy is his inability to get or maintain an erection or because he regularly experiences premature ejaculation. The client is usually prompted to start therapy because he has met someone whom he really likes but fears that, while his new partner has been supportive thus far, he or she will become frustrated and eventually lose patience and interest. Such anxiety further diminishes his self-esteem, exacerbating his inability to perform.

Due to feelings of shame and embarrassment, most of these men avoid sex altogether or any conversation about the problem, using excuses such as being tired or having consumed too much alcohol to draw attention away from the truth. Some attempt intercourse without discussing their concern first, hoping that this time "mind over matter" will work. Still others will over-focus on their partner's pleasure, not dealing with their own.

Of course, all of these strategies are likely to result in failure because they are not based on the truth. Emotional distance between the partners will widen, and the prophecy about breaking-up will be self-fulfilling.

After an initial examination by a physician, I take my client through the steps of intelligent lust, which not only sheds light on the purpose and meaning of his problem, but also naturally eases his shame. Most often, such insight begins to dislodge it. But if the problem persists, I use some of the techniques developed by sexual therapists to deal with the mechanics of sex. I first coach the client on how to have conversations with his partner. Where silence can be divisive, involving a partner in the solution encourages greater intimacy. I suggest exercises couples can do together before they ever attempt to have sex. Often these involve the compatibility exercises suggested in these pages or simple exercises that are more sensual than sexual. I'll often teach my clients how to use specific breathing and relaxation techniques. While some of these techniques may sound cold or clinical, in practice they can be fun and very pleasurable.

Conclusion

S ex is far from the base or primitive instinct that we have been led to believe. It is our most complicated human need. Through it, we connect, communicate, negotiate power, give and receive pleasure, and, sometimes, heal our inner lives.

Our sexual fantasies and desires are windows into the deepest levels of our psyches. By understanding them, we also come to understand our basic personalities, as our minds take our most painful feelings and conflicts and convert them into something pleasurable: What a miraculous phenomenon! And sex is the transformer. Rather than becoming defeated by feelings of isolation, helplessness, invisibility, loneliness, or rejection, we become aroused by them.

Not all sex grows out of conflict, but for the vast majority of us, our sexual fantasies and desires represent the story we tell ourselves to solve deeper issues and satisfy unmet childhood needs. We need to understand and respect these stories if we are to make the best choices for our lives.

For most, fulfilling our fantasies and true desires will lead to greater authenticity and health. Others will be guided to choose mates with whom they will not only experience pleasure, but also create a lasting relationship. For those already in relationships, we will have the opportunity to achieve greater intimacy, honest communication, and a renewed sexual relationship with our partners that brings us to greater spiritual heights.

By completing the steps of intelligent lust, we have experienced the deeper nature of sex. Sex is no longer something one person does to another, nor is it a guessing game or mystery. We have acknowledged the truth about our fantasies and desires, and unearthed hidden conflicts and unmet needs by making important connections to our past. We have created new relationship experiences that foster trust, respect, and intimacy to counteract and repair old conflicted ones and the persistent claim of early unmet needs. We have dared to make sex a vital part of our lives, a rich fertile ground in which we cultivate self-knowledge and self-acceptance.

Embracing our fantasies is not a static experience; our desires slowly unfold over the course of our lifetimes. New desires or preferences will surface when we no longer require the old ones. Because intelligent lust fully engages our senses, minds, and souls, there is always more for us to understand, enjoy, and share. We sublimely discover many truths.

Some of us will follow our desires down entirely new paths, while others remain faithful to the original, even though we have repaired the conflicts from which they sprang. Like a veteran artist, our tastes and inventiveness grow more nuanced with time.

Perhaps it's topsy-turvy, but in the process of forming a restorative relationship, love for a partner may develop. It's likely not to be the blind head-over-heels volatile love as often happens in conventional or new romances. Nor is it built on obligation or responsibility. Instead, it grows gradually and intelligently from friendship as we openly explore our desires with a partner. What we achieve in sharing such an adventure is a special connection—profound, unsentimental, and solid, in which generosity is the central virtue.

Whether or not true love endures as a result, following the steps of intelligent lust is certain to lead us to self-love as we grow to accept, honor, and even celebrate the pain and the pleasure that lead us to a place of deep satisfaction. As Oscar Wilde so aptly put it, "To love oneself is the beginning of a lifelong romance."

Sex lies at the core of our individual identities. We use it to transform pain into pleasure, loneliness into connection, and fear into joy in our indomitable drive to heal past suffering. We all yearn for reconciliation and catharsis.

My hope is that I will help transform our moralistic yet sex-obsessed society to one that appreciates the deeper meaning and value of sex, one person at a time. We can heal from the consequences of shame and guilt and release a new vitality which is based on trust, respect, honesty, and compassion rather than on the aggression which we have collectively eroticized as a nation.

The challenge is for all of us to embrace the deepest and highest levels of our being by giving sex a position in our private and public lives equal to the importance we give to religion. Sex should be at the center of our lives. We should celebrate it because it enlightens us about who we are and who we can become. It is a divining rod that leads to a powerful source of healing energy.

Reread the pages of this book periodically. Complete the exercises again to see how your experience differs a second time. It will help you consolidate what you've learned and perhaps give you new insights into what you have yet to understand.

ALYSSA'S THOUGHTS
The Next Wave

Smart sex is responsible sex. It involves self-knowledge, self-esteem, and respect for our partners. While a restorative experience with a partner has a lot of what are traditionally considered elements of genuine love, such as kindness and generosity, it lacks the irrational swoon that often accompanies the feeling of falling in love. What can be better than experiencing a relationship in which there is not only passion, but also honesty, openness, and trust? And while those qualities may be associated with love, love can also be jealous, possessive, and selfish. A restorative relationship, by definition, cannot be.

Personally, I like the feeling of being in love, that joyous sense of rapture, but at thirty-five, if I had to make a choice, I would seek out a restorative relationship. I believe that genuine and durable love can grow from a restorative relationship, and for myself, I prefer it to grow from such a solid foundation.

My hope is that we will use the ideas expressed in *Your Brain on Sex* to help young people, the future husbands, wives, and parents of our world, learn about sexuality earlier in their lives. We can help teach our children to live more sex-positive lives by our own example.

As we gradually learn to honor and accept who we are as individuals, we will slowly move toward a sex-friendly culture. We can hope for a future with a better balance between genders in which men will view sex and relationships from more of a female perspective and woman will feel, as men do now, more entitled to having and expressing sexual desires.

One final note: As we grow and evolve as people, so does our sexuality. Over time we find some things more attractive, some things less. Our experiences change our chemistry, both what we put out and what we are drawn to. There is always more to understand and experience. Most importantly, enjoy the process. Self-discovery is what keeps our lives meaningful and satisfying and our relationships from growing stale.

About the Author

STANLEY SIEGEL, LCSW, is a psychotherapist in New York City, where he lives. He is an international lecturer and former professor, and he was the director of education and a senior faculty member at New York's renowned Ackerman Institute for Family Therapy. He wrote the "Families" column for *Newsday* and is the coauthor of *The Patient Who Cured His Therapist: And Other Unconventional Stories* (Penguin 1992) and *Unchartered Lives: Understanding the Life Passages of Gay Men* (Penguin 1994). His books have been translated into five languages.

photo credit: Posy Quarterman

ALYSSA SIEGEL, LPC, is a licensed counselor in Portland, Oregon, where she practices individual, couples, and group therapy. Her specialty is women's relationships and sexuality. As a member of the Society for the Scientific Study of Sexuality, she is involved in education and advocacy for women's mental and sexual health and healing. She is currently writing a book on women and body image.